Art Bollockese

fallacies in projecting and promoting Modern Art

Jeff Andrews LLB graduated in Law in 2004 whilst working for a government agency specialising in the examination of dodgy commercial contracts. This involved wading through intellectual guff (*Bollockese*) in order to identify misrepresentation and fraud. In 2008 Jeff opened the *Peche-Art Gallery* in Kent, England, together with Deborah Peche and became the on-call curator. During this period Jeff gained first-hand experience of the changes taking place in the art-world; with contemporary art fashion being influenced by art-intellectuals using high-brow sales pitches to obtain gallery space for artists producing what can only be described as 'unskilled, simplistic or bizarre works'. From his experience examining intellectual babble, Jeff recognised Art was being engulfed in written and verbal dross to 'big-up' simple and crazy concepts. He also recognised some of these works appeared to fall outside the established definitions of 'Art' bringing him to the conclusion; the global populous are now increasingly being visually defrauded by '*Art-Bollockese*'. Jeff is the person behind the commentary of *Joe C Threwitt MA* emphasising the need for Joe Public to see through the high-brow bollockese language used to describe, explain and sale modern art.

Art
Bollockese

fallacies in projecting and promoting modern Art

Jeff Andrews

featuring
Joe C. Threwitt, MA

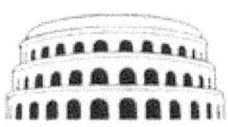

Arena Books

First published in 2019 by Arena Books

Arena Books
6 Southgate Green
Bury St. Edmunds
IP33 2BL

www.arenabooks.co.uk

Distributed in America by Ingram International, One Ingram Blvd., P.O. Box
3006, La Vergne, TN 37086-1985, USA.

Jeff Andrews
Art Bollockese fallacies in projecting and promoting modern Art

British Library cataloguing in Publication Data. A Catalogue record
for this book is available from the British Library.

ISBN-13   978-1-911593-35-5

BIC classifications:- AB, ACVT, ACXD, AFC, AFKB.

Printed and bound by Lightning Source UK

Cover design
By Jason Anscomb

Typeset in
Times New Roman

CONTENTS
Featured Artists & Respective Works

PREFACE

"If you're fed up with art intellectuals telling you how brilliant artworks are that look like they've been created by a child or a tree-climbing primate ... this is the book for you,"

ART – BOLLOCKESE

D on't you just hate it when a mental picture is painted to make you think something is brilliant but then turns out in reality to be absolutely the opposite?

This happens with many things. In politics it's rife, it happens regularly in the work place when bosses want to change things usually to your detriment and of course when someone is trying to sell you something you don't really want. So how is this phoney but believable mental picture achieved? The simple answer is, by dressing it up with 'Bollockese':

Bollockese **unaccountable or singular noun: a noun that has no plural.** *Nonsensical verbiage or high-brow language used to communicate; unproven or biased opinion, or an exaggerated truth; by a person who possesses or has pretensions of superior learning to project or promote items or concepts.* **Definition Source: J. C. Threwitt MA**

Increasingly in our everyday life we are being subject to bollockese, most of which is basically marketing bull or up-themselves academics trying to impress anyone who will listen. This is especially the case in the Art-world which is up there amongst the worst. Art academics spew hyped drivel regularly to Joe Public, so-much-so, art-bollockese can now be expected at nearly every exhibition and especially those exhibiting contemporary works that could have been knocked up by any animal with teeth or digits. This arty bollockese is now so widely accepted, before you are able to view any modern pieces of work, you are required to read 10,000 words of blurb in order to convince you that what you are looking at is great art and not the actual dross exhibited in front of you.

Therefore, to address this issue, this is the first of a series of books championing the return of 'Art Honesty' whereby it is advocated you are allowed to appreciate a piece of artwork without any written explanation or commentary. Only then would you be able to see the artwork in the raw and appreciate its individual true worth. This does not mean that some less skilfully executed pieces can't be appreciated... of course they can... but what now is desperately needed is a major cull of the 'Art

Bollockese' nonsense language academics use to praise or discredit works as they feel fit. You may ask, "Why do they use so much bollockese to analyse art"? The answer now seems obvious to anyone with an iota of sense …It is for self promoting elitism reasons and because those with knowledge or purporting to have knowledge can spout unproven visionary hogwash usually for some form of personal gain.

It is now an established fact; Art in particular has been high-jacked by academics. The norm now being, these intellectuals nearly always use metaphoric high-brow language when critiquing artworks. Is it also true that whenever you visit a gallery or confronted with a so-called piece of nonsense or simplistic art, you know to expect a stream of intellectual art-bollockese describing what you should be viewing and why. As a result; it is now believed these arty-boffins have brought about the dumbing down of art, maybe inadvertently or maybe not, however in doing so they have managed to achieve changes to the definition of Art to include whatever their selective group wishes. Unfortunately this now includes almost anything you can see, hear or feel to the detriment of any skill or common sense perceptions. Accordingly, over-time these individuals who have become masters of the craft of bollockese, have therefore been able to direct art-fashion by promoting what they feel should be appreciated. This position of influence being afforded to them by the myth; '*If they are academics they must be credible*'. Within the world of Art this seems particularly the case, as the art-academic establishment successfully dictate who the good artists are and why we should appreciate their sometimes crazy concepts. Accordingly, anyone commenting on a public platform not recognised by the established art academia is made to feel they lack the appreciative awareness to make a valid critique. Basically they are 'numtyfied' by being drowned in posturing arty-bla-bla abuse and the claim they lack the artistic vision to understand the bollockese being spouted.

Okay there are a number of things that now seem clear; (i) We the so-called masses, are being hood-winked by the art-boffins in order to like what they want us to like. (ii) It's also fair to claim; the artworks increasingly championed by these self-determined visionaries are being produced by a selected type of artist, who have been embraced by influential sections of this elitist group….and (iii) It seems reasonable to suggest; some artists have been elevated to heights far greater than they deserve by interested parties in the art-world utilising art-bollockese hype.

Furthermore, it is noticeable the chosen fortunate few, appear to be able to produce artworks on demand, therefore ideal for modern-day marketing and gallery exhibition purposes. The most likely reason for this is the marketing gurus have found there is only so much you can make out of technically adept artists as they are usually pedantic and therefore slow in their creations. However, if you can popularise someone producing simplistic art and prolific, or even better a known celebrity in other fields who dabbles in art, you have yourself a regenerating money tree. Cynical may-be, but come on we all really know it's the truth!

Given this obvious thus valid scepticism of how art is currently portrayed to the general public, the aim here is to reclaim the standing of true art and not be taken in by the guff and pure art-bollockese we are made to endure to influence our appreciation.

Therefore, what we are trying to achieve is to simply bring back some common sense into Art, by advocating the reliance of your own senses to view artworks without explanation or commentary. Art will then become honest, with clarity of value, expressed by your own appreciation of a piece. In short a row of traffic cones are just that; 'a row of traffic cones' or a light flashing on and off is what it is…Not Art! We all really know this, so ask yourselves, "Why the hell are we being influenced by these so-called art-experts because they have attained a pass mark in some 'ology'"? And come on, we also really know; those who embark on studies for an ology are required to babble incessantly and write thousands of words, when ten will do.

No one's knocking these academic boffins for wanting to use their educated higher status to earn a crust, but using it to hoodwink others less knowing, is just wrong. Just take a look on the internet you will find a web-site called; *'The Instant Art Critique Phrase Generator'*. The apparent purpose of this web-site is to assist the so-called art-experts when they get stuck for bollockese. The fact that this nonsense dictionary exists, surely means its now time this art balderdash is reigned in as we are clearly losing any sense of visual truth. If this distortion of art continues the art-world will become la-la-land… and let's face it; we are already there, with some of the following examples chosen proving this beyond any doubt to those of us with any iota of common sense.

Having pondered how to deal with this distortion of truth in art, it is felt a white-knight is needed to champion the reasonable views of 'Joe Public'. That white-knight has now been found to speak out for us like-minded dissenters to the dictatorial supercilious art establishment and the bollockese they inflict upon us.

Therefore, please let me introduce the fictional: **Joe C. Threwitt MA.** The 'MA' does not stand-for 'Master of Arts' but 'Master of Acumen'. Joe henceforth will become our nominated champion of common sense.

Joe C. Threwitt MA, believes in the true meaning of Art that requires some form of artistic skill which is felt to be important in determining the true worth of any artwork. Unfortunately the art-bollockese academics have already denounced the word 'classical' to portray something that is 'old fashioned'. Also the definition of what is determined as 'Art' has now been bastardized to accept basically anything that can be produced, however ridiculous. This perception of what should now be accepted as Art, being orchestrated and thrust upon us by the art-marketing gurus and their intellectual flunkies. These boffins claiming to be experts, gush their bullshit art-bollockese in order to convince us whatever they say, write or comment on, is the general view of the art establishment and therefore something that should be embraced by us all.

Joe C Threwitt MA, therefore advocates that artworks should truly remain within the boundaries of what was accepted before recent intellectual influences. Accordingly, to be determined as Art, works must retain all three components as per the following definitions obtained from two credible sources. One American and the other British, so you don't think this is a sole Brit conspiracy.

Merriam-Webster Dictionary – Definition of Art:
*Art is **something that is created with [1] imagination** and **[2] skill** and that is **[3] beautiful or that expresses important ideas or feelings***

Oxford Dictionary – Definition of Art:
*Art is the expression or **application of [1] human creative skill** and **[2] imagination, typically in a visual form** such as painting or sculpture, producing works to be **appreciated primarily for their [3] beauty or emotional power.***

So there you have it; to be considered a piece of Art, the artwork must incorporate three elements, not one, not two, but all three. It is on this basis *Joe C. Threwitt MA* will make comment with the intention of introducing a balanced, reasonable and common-sense perspective on contemporary art pieces. The chosen pieces have been critiqued and accepted by those now dictating what we the great-unwashed should recognise as being great art. In doing so, they have used elaborate chunks of art-bollockese to justify their jumped-up opinionated claims. This now seeming the norm with artworks being praised by so-called art-experts, leaving people with 20/20 vision and some form of measured thinking absolutely dumbfounded

Nevertheless, it has to be accepted 'Art' like 'Beauty' is very much in the eye of the beholder. It also has to be said Joe's following comments are not so much about the featured artists, but the art-bollockese that have influenced their works worth. Therefore, Joe C. Threwitt's comments should be taken with this in mind. The aim of the commentary is not to inhibit the creation of art-works but to shine a humorous but poignant light on some odd-ball works that some people like for whatever reason. However, what is also true; there is a silent global mass of people out there, which like our fictitious commentator fail to recognise some of the following featured pieces as 'Art' for equally good reasons.

Having considered the staggering amount of dross-art out there, being claimed to the contrary by those purporting to be in the know, it seems appropriate to start with the work exhibited back in 1974, in what is the highly acclaimed UK gallery namely: *The Tate Modern*. This work was created, albeit the word 'created' is laughable, by **Carl Andre**, and clearly highlights how ridiculous and bizarre the art establishment has become. Although at the time many did question the sanity of the art-boffins for not only exhibiting Mr Andre's **'Pile of Bricks'**, but these recognised pillars of the art-world apparently allowed the state sponsored gallery to purchase these bricks for 30 times their face value on behalf of you and me.

In order to convince the world these bricks were something to be viewed as artistic and something that holds meaningful expressionism, bollockese was employed by any so-called reputable art-intellectual that could be brought on side by the *Tate*. Arguably, the result has been the demise of credible Art, with the requirement for any element of skill eliminated. Accordingly, Mr Andre's pile of bricks is viewed by *Joe C. Threwitt MA* as: The beginning of the end of sanity in art.

THE BOOK'S FORMAT: First there is a short biography and example of the chosen artist works. Then we will look at facts embellished by bollockese written about the so-called Art and Artists by acknowledged art-intellectuals. This will then be followed by the champion of common sense Joe C Threwitt's comments, which cut through the high-brow bollockese being thrust upon us. So to begin, we will start with the works of *Carl Andre* followed by works of his fellow artists with their respective promotional bollockese....With *Joe C. Threwitt MA* pulling the common sense punches that are far-too-long overdue:

CHAPTER 1

CARL ANDRE

C arl Andre is an American minimalist artist recognized for his ordered linear format and grid format sculptures. His sculptures range from large public artworks to more intimate tile patterns arranged on the floor of an exhibition space.

Born: 16 September 1935, Quincy, Massachusetts, United States
Artwork: Steel Aluminum Plain, 144 Lead Square, Hour Rose, 4 Blocks and Stones, AL Ravine, Pivot
Periods: Contemporary Art, Minimalism
Awards: Guggenheim Fellowship for Creative Arts, US & Canada
Source Wikipedia

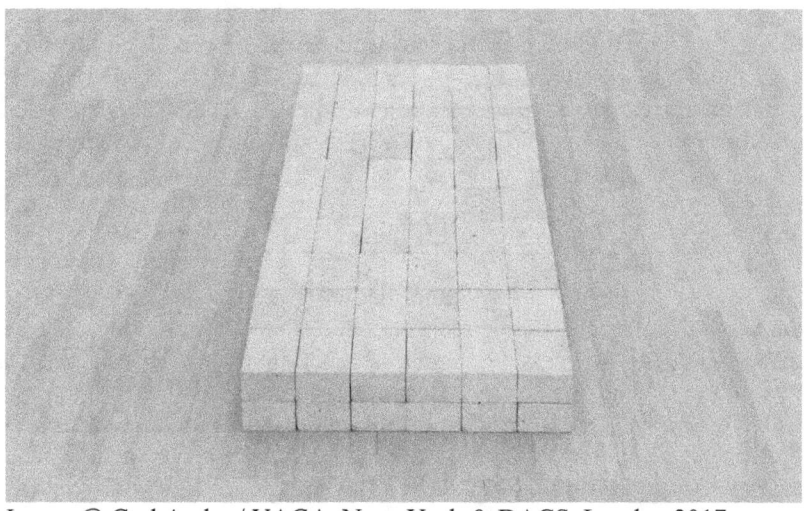

Image @ Carl Andre / VAGA, New York & DACS, London 2017.

Equivalent VIII 1966
(*Better known as: 'The Pile of Bricks'*)

Displayed at Tate Modern UK
Medium Firebricks
Dimensions Object: 127 x 686 x 2292 mm
Collection Tate Acquisition Purchased 1972 for £3000
(Value today equates to approx. £30,000)

EXAMPLES of ART-BOLLOCKESE*:-

Comments from 'Art Experts' re. The Work's of CARL ANDRE:

'The New Yorker' On-line Art Column - "The Materialist" December 5, *2011*:

"…It is hard to think of an artist whose career has been so affected by circumstances that have nothing to do with his art. In (Carl) Andre's case, the precipitating event was the death of his third wife, Ana Mendieta, a young artist who fell from the bedroom window of Andre's apartment, on the thirty-fourth floor of a high-rise on Mercer Street, in the early-morning hours of September 8, 1985. Andre was charged with murder, indicted, and eventually acquitted in a non-jury trial, but Mendieta's family and many of her friends in the art community and the feminist movement believe that he was responsible for her death….

….Wherever Andre was, he kept working. Andre has described himself as the first post-studio artist. He has never needed a studio, because the materials he works with—four-by-four timbers, bricks, one-foot-square metal plates, cut or natural stones, and other available hardware—are ordered from suppliers and assembled by Andre on the site. Andre does not carve, or model, or weld, or transform his materials. His great innovation was to assemble the elements of his simple, linear sculptures on the floor, without joining them together.

Other contemporary sculptors had done away with pedestals and the vertical axis, but Andre's reorientation of his work to the horizontal plane, where it functioned not as an object but, in his words, "as a place," was more radical and more influential than anything being done by Donald Judd, Robert Morris, Dan Flavin, or the other minimalist artists in the nineteen-sixties. "Carl has the floor," as the art crowd at Max's Kansas City used to say. Richard Serra, who is four years younger than Andre, remembers a conversation he had with him soon after Andre's first flat metal-plate pieces were shown at the Dwan gallery in New York, in 1967: "I said to Carl, 'Somebody's got to get those things up off the ground,' and Carl said, 'Don't worry, somebody else will do that.' And I

---

* **BOLLOCKESE** - Nonsensical verbiage or high-brow language used to communicate; unproven or biased opinion or an exaggerated truth; by a person who possesses or has pretensions of superior learning to project or promote items or concepts.

thought, God damn, I'm going to do it!" Soon afterward, Serra started making his freestanding lead-prop sculptures, in which four massive, upright lead plates support each other without joints, house-of-cards style. "Carl was an enormous influence on me," Serra said. "He changed the history of sculpture."

The fact that you can walk on Andre's sculptures still confuses viewers. Andre has allowed and encouraged it—with certain reservations. He doesn't want you walking on his metal plates in stiletto heels, or in cleated boots that have snow on them, or with bare feet, whose oils can be more corrosive than rock salt, but he knows that these and other harmful actions will take place. "I stop worrying about what happens to a work after it's out of my control," he said to me. Most museum goers don't walk on his pieces. Even if they know it's allowed, walking on a certified work of art seems transgressive, or showoffy, but the knowledge that you can do it establishes a strong physical connection between spectator and art work. Andre's things have always struck me as inviting the kind of spectator involvement and empathy that early minimalism prided itself on ruling out. When he started making art, he once said, his goal was to make something impersonal and complete in itself, but he found that this was impossible, because "the essence of art is human association." ..."

Article from 'The Paris Review' - "Objects Are What We Aren't"
February 26, 2015 :

(This article, although not directly about Equivalent VIII, refers to another similar installation of a pile of bricks created by Carl Andre)

"...The objects here appear less than entirely concerned with a viewer's emotional state. But indifference is not disdain, and walking around them can offer consolation, if that is what one seeks. Walking *on* them, too—as the showgoer is encouraged to do with certain of Andre's sculptures laid flat on the floor—makes for certain peculiarities of mood. In the exhibition catalogue, curator Yasmil Raymond writes of Andre's habit for evoking the "solemnity and intimacy typically reserved for monuments, graveyards, tombs, and shrines, thus transforming the experience of art into a visit to a 'place' where one enacts an unrepeatable event."

Andre's favored media include steel, iron, copper, lead, zinc, magnesium, hay, and blocks of wood, among many other things. In the early sixties, his declarative arrangements of them guided what would come to be known as minimalism, with their ability to conjure so much by such minimal means. An arrangement of things on the floor, laid out with the right mix of meticulousness and deference to the inner life of materials, could communicate. It could spread and sprawl and have an invisible height to it, or at least suggest a sense of rising into space that needn't be sullied by actually, literally, being risen into. It could define and command space without necessarily occupying it, all by intimation.

Andre's art also, more simply, abides. While finding his way as a sculptor, he worked as a brakeman and conductor for the Pennsylvania Railroad, and his handle on materials is anything but dainty. Sculptures with titles like *Uncarved Blocks* or *Copper-Aluminum Plain* are just that. One of the thrills of the Dia:Beacon show is relaxing into the pure, simple earthiness of the materials on display: rusting steel, cracked wood, sand-lime brick shedding dust on the floor, bars of droopy aluminum. Andre's eye for the arresting aspects of such things can be seen in *Quincy*, a stark and resounding artist book he made in 1973. Its pages are on display at Dia:Beacon, and it was reissued last year by Primary Information. The slim volume is nothing but photographs of industrial environmental scenes around Quincy, Massachusetts, where Andre grew up among granite mines and shipyards. Tumbles of rock and railroad ties abound, with a curious sort of poetry about them. ..."

Article from www.interviewmagazine.com - Published 06/17/13 :

"...(Carl) Andre's accumulations of untransformed materials can also be interpreted as a critique of sculpture itself—particularly its relationship to the verticality of the human body. Rather than confront the spectator with the traditional abstraction that mirrors the viewer's own upright body, Andre organizes his modular arrangements horizontally. To see his work, you must look neither straight ahead nor up, as colossal public sculpture forces you to do, but down. This can be a disorienting experience. You are, in a sense, up to your ankles (and more occasionally your knees) in a Carl Andre.

Andre does not seek to engulf the spectator but to mark off his turf: he wants not intimacy but respect, which is the last thing given to artists when their work is immediately converted into a trading commodity. His metal plates hug the floor even more tenaciously than a carpet since they are glued to nothing—they can be picked up at will just as his pieces made of stacked wooden building planks can easily be disassembled.....

.....The common feature of Andre's work is its provisionality—i.e., the fact that it exists as sculpture only at the time it is exhibited. Our knowledge of its precarious and temporary state, as well as our sense that the works can easily revert to their ordinary function, is part of their elusive content. Given its dual identity of being and potentially not being, Andre's work clearly has a strong conceptual element, even though he was making it as far back as 1960, before conceptual art became a popular mind game. (In fact, I remember him calling for a "contraceptual" art at the time.)

For Andre is able to demonstrate without academic explanation Bishop Berkeley's observation that if a tree falls in the forest and no one hears it, then, for the purposes of empiricism, the tree did not fall. However, unlike Berkeley's "immaterialism," Andre claims no spiritual dimension in his art. Whether organized as sculpture or mutely stacked, his pieces maintain their identity as untransformed matter, thus proving Andre's contention that he is a pure materialist. But not without ambiguity, which is why they maintain their tension and fascination…."

 JOE C.THREWITT re. The Work's of CARL ANDRE:

The day in the 1970's when a renowned UK gallery forked out three grand for a pile of 120 fire-bricks on the pretext they were quality art, was the day the art establishment became governed by art-intellectual craziness. From that date, the art-bollockese talking-up such 'off-the-wall' art has seemingly escalated, resulting in the creeping demise of any creative artwork requiring elements of skill.

If you believe this is not true, just wander into any modern gallery and you'll be guaranteed to find something senseless, stupid or weird forced in your face with some intellectual bollockese bigging it up. When Mr Andre's pile of bricks first appeared at this highly respected gallery, yes there was a stink kicked up by those still possessing some common sense. Nevertheless, conceptual craziness gradually won the day with advocates gushing their intellectual art-bollockese drivel, which sadly now has become the art-world norm. This is why those who had influence at this relevant time should hold their heads in shame. As this was the day art involving refined quality and skill hit the buffers.

Anyhow, let's try and be objective about Mr Andre's 'Pile of Bricks'… I think most people would agree, being a builder is an honourable profession. Full of 'salt-of-the-earth' chaps doing a hard day's graft possible laying some 1000 plus bricks in between tea-breaks. These guys lay these bricks with the necessary precision to ensure your des-res walls are built straight and true in the hope they will last a life-time. Skilled bricklayers possess technical ability in basic trigonometry and great hand-to-eye coordination. The result of their endeavours, are often seen as amazing depending upon the architect's design to which they are applying their skills.

However, before any bricklayer can go about his trade, the bricks have to be delivered on-site in a piled stack... *can you see where I'm going with this*. The bricks emanate usually from a builder's yard, stacked in piles by a labourer most likely earning a minimum wage. The reason why the person who only stacks the bricks is on the minimum wage, unlike the skilled bricklayer, is because there is little or no skill in stacking a pile of bricks. Therefore, a person who stacks bricks is globally recognised as being a 'Labourer' not an 'Artist'...unless of course you are a paid up art-intellectual from planet *Tate*.

So, the question that screams out here is; "When does a stack of building material change from being as they are intended, *a stack of building material* to an acclaimed piece of artistic work?" The answer lies directly at the door of the art establishment commentators and in this case those actively commentating on behalf of the *Tate Modern Gallery*. Having searched for some reasoning in this matter, like many, I am at a loss to find some logic or sense as to why the main-man at the *Tate* would give the nod to pay 30 times the face value for a stack of bricks from an alleged murder suspect. And having done so, have the gall to think Joe Public would actually be impressed and believe a stack of bricks piled up by a joker called Andre is a marvellous piece of Art, worthy of exhibition and acclaim.

Cue the art-bollockese. The art-boffins who championed Mr Andre's bricks had to dig really deep into their descriptive blurb to make this exhibit palatable. It beggars belief that these clever arty-individuals are really talking about a pile of building material when they comment: "...*The objects here appear less than entirely concerned with a viewer's emotional state. But indifference is not disdain, and walking around them can offer consolation, if that is what one seeks. Walking on them, too—as the showgoer is encouraged to do with certain of Andre's sculptures laid flat on the floor—makes for certain peculiarities of mood....*"

Not something you often hear on a building site.. why?.. Because it's absolute bonkers bollockese. Imagine Bob-the-Builder wandering around his pile of bricks spouting this stuff... I think his work colleagues would have something to say beginning with 'F' and ending with 'Off'. Nevertheless, lets examine Mr Andre's 'Pile of Bricks' to see if they can be considered a true work of 'Art' as per the definitions:

Does piling bricks on top of one-and-other shows imagination?... Ha..you must be kidding...The only imagination shown here is that of the exhibition curators who somehow managed to pull this stunt off. So that's a NO for Mr Andre but an amazing YES for the bollockese boys!

Does piling up these bricks require some skilled technical ability?... Well I suppose you need some basic hand-to-eye coordination. Who am I kidding; of course there's little or no skill in creating this excuse for Art. Any kindergarten school attendee could put one row of bricks on-top of another. If there is any skill here, it must be awarded to engineers at Vitcas or some other Firebrick manufacturer. Therefore it must be said, with regard to Mr Andre's creation displaying some skill or technical ability, that's another NO!...

What about something of beauty or express feelings / ideas of importance?... I can't even be bothered to answer this one as it's so obvious to any person with reasonable sight or nous these bricks aren't beautiful or mean jack to anyone without any linked monetary interest.

So, to sum things up; Mr Andre's 'Pile of Bricks' just don't stack up (excuse the pun) as being a work of 'Art' as per the recognised definitions. However, what ceases to amaze is; although the bollockese spouted about these bricks was so utterly ridiculous and laughable, no one in the art-higher-echelons said, "wait-stop, this is absolute nonsense!" It therefore seems apparent, this decision by the UK art-establishment had a foreseeable consequence; if the public acquiesce to a stack of bricks being fit for artistic exhibition, then in future there now exists an acknowledged acceptance that trash-art lacking skill is the way forward....and evidently so it has been.

Joe's Quote of Note for Mr Andre and his 'Pile of Bricks':
"Controversy is the last resort of the talent less" **Criss Jami, Healolog**

CHAPTER 2

TRACEY EMIN

T racey Emin, CBE, RA (born 3 July 1963) is an English contemporary artist known for her autobiographical and confessional artwork. ... Once the "enfant terrible" of the Young British Artists in the 1980s, Tracey Emin is now a Royal Academician of the Royal Academy of Arts.

In 1997, her work; *Everyone I Have Ever Slept With 1963–1995*, a tent appliquéd with the names of everyone the artist had ever shared a bed with was shown at Charles Saatchi's Sensation exhibition held at the Royal Academy in London. The same year, she gained considerable media exposure when she swore multiple times in a state of drunkenness on a live discussion programme called; *The Death of Painting* on British television.

In December 2011, she was appointed Professor of Drawing at the Royal Academy;.. she is one of the first two female professors since the Academy was founded in 1768. *Source Wikipedia.*

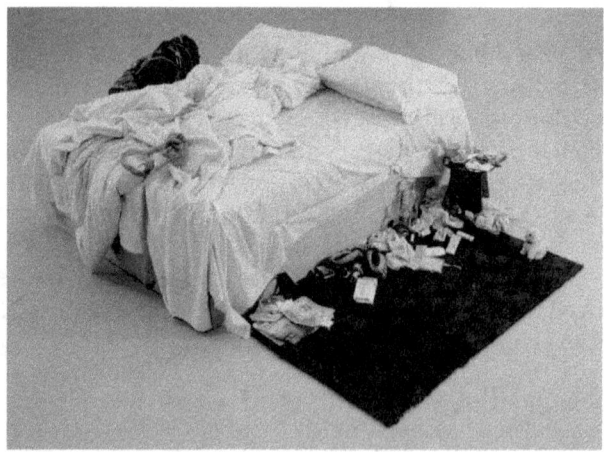

Image @ Saatchi Gallery

Tracey Emin - 'My Bed' (1998)
Mattress, Linens, Pillows, Objects
79 x 211 x 234 cm
Purchase Price: £2.54 Million

EXAMPLES of ART-BOLLOCKESE*:-

Comments from 'Art Experts' re. The Work's of TRACEY EMIN:

Tate (UK) Gallery Catalogue Commentary - Tracey Emin's 'My Bed':
"A consummate storyteller, Tracey Emin engages the viewer with her candid exploration of universal emotions. Well-known for her confessional art, Tracey Emin reveals intimate details from her life to engage the viewer with her expressions of universal emotions. Her ability to integrate her work and personal life enables Emin to establish an intimacy with the viewer.

Tracey shows us her own bed, in all its embarrassing glory. Empty booze bottles, fag butts, stained sheets, worn panties: the bloody aftermath of a nervous breakdown...."

Evening Standard Art Columnist Wednesday 27th May 2009 :

" I have always loved Tracey Emin's bed (without ever dreaming of sharing it). My Bed was part of her room at the 1999 Turner Prize show, the year she was shortlisted but didn't win. I liked its dirty sheets, overflowing ashtrays, used condoms and empty bottles.

Dissenters told me this was the work of a lazy artist with a hangover who couldn't get up in the morning. But it had an artistic logic. The Bed was like one of those photos of a junkie's messy bedroom by a documentary photographer, someone like Nan Goldin. It had a political power, too. It was a taboo-busting feminist sculpture that turned the image of a woman-as-harlot into harlot-as-heroine, and it seemed, rather handily, to suggest a future with a lot more opportunities for men, too. It wasn't what men expected liberated women to be, but nor was it what orthodox feminists wanted women to be either...... "

The Mail Online Art Columnist 30 March 2015 :

" Artist Tracey Emin wiped away tears as she unveiled her £2.54 million unmade bed - complete with discarded condoms - on its return to its "home" at the Tate. My Bed became notorious when it was shortlisted for

---

* **BOLLOCKESE** - Nonsensical verbiage or high-brow language used to communicate; unproven or biased opinion or an exaggerated truth; by a person who possesses or has pretensions of superior learning to project or promote items or concepts.

the Turner Prize and displayed at Tate Britain in 1999. Over 15 years later, it is back at the gallery on a long-term loan for at least 10 years....

...Emin admitted that unlike the chaotic-looking installation, which features empty vodka bottles, cigarette butts, stained sheets and discarded underwear, her bed at home is now a different affair. "I make my bed every day. It's so boring, it's very neat. I'm really OCD (obsessive compulsive disorder)," she said. Wiping away tears, the artist said that seeing the work - which is now subject to rigorous security in the form of a sensor and a guard to prevent visitors from getting too close - left her emotional....

...The work, which expressed the artist's suicidal depression following a relationship breakdown, is displayed in its own room alongside two paintings by Francis Bacon and six nude drawings by Emin which she has given to the Tate. Emin said she felt validated seeing the installation on display alongside works by some of Britain's "greats" after all the criticism about the bed at the time....

....Tate director commented: "It's a work we've always wanted to bring into the collection.... It was quite clear from 1999 when it was first seen in the Turner prize that it was going to be regarded as one of those iconic works from the late 90s." The "really important work" was being given "a historical dimension", he added as "part of the story of British art over a long period".

The work fetched £2.54 million at auction, a record for the artist, when it was purchased by dealer and White Cube gallery owner Jay Jopling last year.

(Tracey Emin's 'My Bed' was originally bought by Millionaire collector Charles Saatchi for £150,000 in 2000 and was sold via Christie's Art Auctioneers)..."

Tate Gallery Curator's Comments 30 March 2015 :

" It's wonderful to have it (My Bed) back at the Tate and Tracey was very thrilled to have My Bed coming back here. It is a very important moment for her as an artist as well as for us as an institution," she said. "It's a new moment for My Bed and a moment to reassess it. It is not just about the media hype, it is about looking at the formal qualities of the work and thinking about the work in more historical terms alongside other major figures."

The Tate Britain Curator added: "It is a very different cultural presentation of the work. In 1999, it was displayed as part of the Turner prize, so it was all about being fresh and new, whereas this time, the desire was to contextualise My Bed as part of 700 years of British art and is displayed alongside other works in the permanent collection. So, we discussed this with Tracey and what would be the most suitable companions, and she was involved in selecting the paintings that would be shown alongside her work. Francis Bacon was a very immediate answer, because there are wonderful reference's between their works. There is this sheer vitality of the body that moves in spaces combined with a sense of internal turmoil. I think the coupling really works very well.….

….I think it certainly holds its power and it was a wonderful experience to see it literally unfold in the room," she said. "It's still an incredibly vital piece but the main difference now is that it has become a very significant piece in the trajectory of a now very established British artist. So, I think the status of the work has changed historically but certainly hasn't changed in terms of the impact of the piece…"

 JOE C.THREWITT re. The Work's of TRACEY EMIN:

Well.. there you have it, some examples of art-bollockese at its very best in relation to Ms Emin's 'My Bed'. Ms Emin whose relatively recent celebrity status is believed to be due to marketing gurus Saatchi & Saatchi's 'extra-ordinary' support. She has produced many pieces that could be considered within this book, but lets start with '*My Bed*' which is probably her most recognised piece'….Crikey! where do you start with the self-styled queen of human detritus. Okay probably the best way of bringing some common sense to the table…sorry bed… is to see if the piece being described by the commentating art-intellectuals as great Art, can actually be determined as Art.

So is it a creation that shows imagination?….
     It certainly is a creation.. but one assumes initially it was an accidental creation due to this supposed sense of turmoil Ms Emin was feeling at that time. However, it can reasonably be said there was no imagination in the production of the piece. Nevertheless, Ms Emin or someone conspiring with her definitely imagined it could be worth a bob-or-two if the art world could be convinced her messy bed held some deep sociological meaning...Bring on the bollockese…and so inevitably they

did, probably with the help of Mr Saatchi's expert marketing bollock-geezers.

Does the creation of 'My Bed' require skill or involve some technical ability?

Ha.ha. Now this is definitely a no-brainer .... Okay let's try and be objective and find something positive…It seems reasonable to suppose, having decided the messy bed could become something of value, you would have to be able to re-create it or at-least preserve its original state… Or would you? Who would know one messy bed from another, or indeed care if one pair of skiddy knickers or used condom was placed here or there.

Anyhow let's say when originally exhibiting the piece, it had to be reconstructed…Whoa! Hang on I'm drifting into bollockese myself here… this is absolute nonsense… and as my old dad would say "Even with bells and whistles, crap is still crap, but with bells and whistles." It's pretty obvious to anyone with a modicum of sense; even competent exponents of bollockese would have difficulty sorting this mess to find any skill, let alone any technical ability in executing the creation of 'My Bed'. Basically, you could sling any old female dross over and beside the bed and it would basically achieve the same outcome.. a messy bed!..

Does the piece portray something of beauty or express feelings / ideas of importance?

Well I think I can write off 'My Bed' being visually pleasurable to the average man riding the omnibus. Therefore, that leaves us with the question of whether the piece expresses any feelings or ideas of importance…

I'm going to be really kind here to Ms Emin and go along with her comments of how her messy bed expressed how she felt at that time in her life… albeit pains me to do so. With regard to ideas of importance: The only true importance of the piece is held by Ms Emin herself. Any bollockese to the contrary, should be taken for what it is…absolute nonsense! Nevertheless, that does exclude those in the art marketing business wishing to make some spondulicks from the piece. Therefore to try and give this piece some sociological deep construction is more than bollockese, and any person with an honest soul should disregard such hype for what it is… pure and utter tosh!

Now let's just be clear about the bollockese here. There certainly are some classic quotes. For example, "*…consummate story teller*", "*…embarrassing glory*" and that old favourite "*…artistic logic*". Who would ever guess these words would be used to describe Ms Emin's '*My Bed*'. Oh yes not forgetting...there always has to be an analogy, however oblique. So with '*My Bed*' an analogy to the works of an equally off the wall photographer Nan Goldin has been thrown in. The claim here being both Goldin and Emin's works holds some political power relative to feminist statements or not.. Ehhh...confused.. you bet! So what seems clear here is; the artistic cleverness is not actually Ms Emin's slovenly lifestyle piece, but the bollockese literal efforts promoting it.

It has to be said; most bollockese statements are used by academic commentators to promote anything that is undistinguishable requiring a marketing push. This could be a piece of so-called art, as it is here, or anything such as dilapidated piece of real estate or a celebrity chef's dish of the day. It means 'jack'. You are being asked to join imaginary dots to form a picture in your mind, which lets face it in most cases bares no resemblance to what you are looking at.

And how about this bollockese summing up by a gallery curator...who of course has no bias interest in the piece (*not arrf*)...although his continued employment relies on it. At least the gallery had the sense not to directly charge the public for the privilege of viewing the piece. Anyhow, on behalf of the gallery he claims: *"It's still an incredibly vital piece but the main difference now is that it has become a very significant piece in the trajectory of a now very established British artist. So, I think the status of the work has changed historically but certainly hasn't changed in terms of the impact of the piece."* Bla..bla blaa..Who the hell are they kidding...Yep that's right...You!

Okay so where are we with this..; '*My Bed*' has now been viewed from what has to be a reasonable common sense perspective with examination against two globally accepted definitions of what is to be determined as Art.. What now appears conclusive is; Tracey Emin's '*My Bed*' definitely falls short of any skill in creation. The definition would also have to be 'twisted' to include any other of the requisite components to make '*My Bed*' a piece of Art, in its true sense. Therefore, it is concluded by this commentator: '*My Bed*' is as much a work of Art as my left boot when I've stood in dog pooh...But wait... Maybe with a big dollop of bollockese from the art establishment so-called intellectuals, that too may be worth a couple of £Million.

Joe's Quote of Note for Ms Emin and '*My Bed*": *"A messy bed is a trivial thing but getting rid of clutter gives a disproportionate boost to happiness"* **Gretden Ruben**

CHAPTER 3

MARTIN CREED

Martin Creed was born in 1968 in Wakefield, England. From the age of three he lived in Glasgow, Scotland. Between 1986 and 1990 he studied at the Slade School of Fine Art, London. After art school he lived and worked in London until 2001, when he moved to Alicudi, Italy. In 2001 he was the winner of the Turner Prize.
Source Wikipedia.

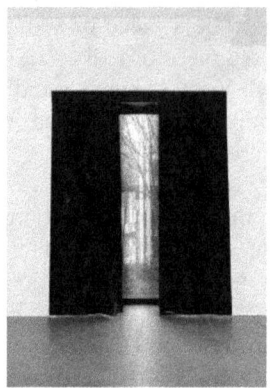

Images @ www. martincreed.com

Martin Creed - Work No. 990
Curtains opening and closing - 2009

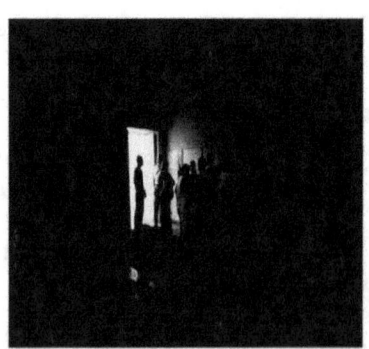 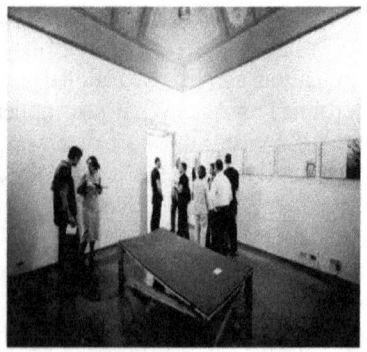

Martin Creed - Work No. 227 (1995)
The lights going on and off
Dimensions variable; 30 seconds on / 30 seconds off

EXAMPLES of ART- BOLLOCKESE*:-

Comments from 'Art Experts' re. The Work's of MARTIN CREED:

Article by Art Critic; Maurizio Cattelan (2004):

" We all have our bad days, when you just can't get it right, like moments of loss and surrender. And we all have our good days, when everything seems to run smoothly, just perfect for no apparent reason. I can see clearly now the rain has gone. You wake up, things are okay, and the sun is shining. And then out of the blue, there you go again, down into the dark pit of depression. It's not just a matter of mood swings. Its something more basic and perverse: the inability to preserve joy.

The need to measure it against a black background. Art is no different. It's a ride on the roller coaster of emotions. Sometimes I feel so happy, sometimes I feel so sad. I always thought Martin Creed's *Work: The lights going on and off* had something to do with this simple truth. It has the ability to compress happiness and anxiety within one single gesture. Lights go on, lights go off – sunshine and rain, and then back to beginning to repeat endlessly. I do not know what Creed was thinking about when he made it but to me it always looked like a swing, a mood swing. That's why I never found it funny but frightening in its simplicity, it's a sculpture for our lithium oriented, Prozac enhanced reality. Are we afraid of the dark or just blinded by the light? I see a rainbow and I want to paint it black…"

Article by Art Critic; Mark Hudson - 27 Jan 2014 :

"There's a double-bluffing simplicity to Martin Creed's work, with its numbered titles and bluntly explanatory tags, that appears designed to wind-up the non-expert viewer.

Take his Turner Prize-winning Work 227 The lights Going on and off. Comprising simply the lights going on and off in an empty gallery, it remains the Turner-winning work most likely to annoy the man in the

---

* **BOLLOCKESE** - Nonsensical verbiage or high-brow language used to communicate; unproven or biased opinion or an exaggerated truth; by a person who possesses or has pretensions of superior learning to project or promote items or concepts.

street because of its perceived clever-cleverness: is it intended to be profound or is it nothing more than it appears to be?

If that work was startlingly minimal, the effect on entering his most extensive retrospective to date at the Hayward Gallery is startlingly maximal. Clambering over Work 142 A large piece of furniture partially obstructing a door which is just a battered leather sofa plonked in the doorway, you find Work 1357 Mothers, a massive revolving iron beam, looming alarmingly overhead (I won't give any more work numbers from this point). Surmounted by the word Mothers, spelled out in six foot high neon letters, it seems to imply that our maternal parents are threatening as well as nurturing. A soundtrack is provided by the clatter of 39 metronomes all running at different speeds...

...Creed and other artists of his generation – the so-called YBAs – have benefited greatly from general ignorance of late 20th century art. Indeed, while his work has been projected by the media as offering a wincing shock of the new (and he hasn't, in fairness, made such claims himself), there is virtually nothing here that hasn't been done before. The American artist George Brecht did a work with cars turning their lights on and off in 1962. Creed's stacks of iron girders hark back to Seventies minimalism. Bodily fluids were done to death decades ago by the Viennese Actionists.

If the work doesn't break new ground, what we're left with is its relative visual interest and its entertainment value. Creed, apparently, doesn't consider himself a minimalist or a conceptualist – as you would assume – but an expressionist, dealing with feelings and atmospheres. Yet if the work touches on his personal history and phobias this is hardly available by looking at it.

Creed essentially is a showman with an instinct for the stylishly provocative gesture. Film of a penis tumescing and detumesching is undoubtedly juvenile, but showing it on an external terrace, framed against the Shell Centre and the London Eye, took a chutzpah you can't help admiring. Half the air in a given space, in contrast, an enclosure of helium-filled white balloons, which the viewer is encouraged to clamber through, belongs in the same territory of quite entertaining, family-friendly contemporary art as Jeremy Deller's bouncy-castle Stonehenge.

Best of all is Curtains opening and closing, a pair of black curtains (surprise, surprise) opening and closing to reveal a purposeless monolith, placed on the terrace against the London skyline. The two separate works perfectly complement each other in this context, the layers of industrial brick evoking the textures of the surrounding urban landscape.

This piece feels resonant in a way most of the other work here doesn't. Creed's is an art of smart ideas, but you leave the Hayward feeling there aren't quite enough of them to fill a gallery of this size…"

 JOE C.THREWITT re. The Work's of MARTIN CREED:

Ha..ha… Well what do you reckon on this load of bollockese then. Don't you just love the bit about *"double-bluffing simplicity.."* and *"annoying..the man in the street.."* due to Mr Creeds *"..perceived clever – cleverness…".* How bloody condescending and what seems simply amazing, is how these so-called art intellectuals are not laughed out of the room. Probably it's because they purposely avoid direct communication with anyone who would tell them the truth...namely the man in the street! Anyhow, let's see how these pieces sit with being categorised as works of 'Art':

Does these creations show imagination?....
Well I think they certainly show some form of creation. At least on the part of the electric light and curtain manufacturers. Nevertheless, these manufactured creations were never meant to be considered to be artistic. Simply functional for life's purposes of seeing when dark and keeping ones privacy after dusk. With regard to possessing *imagination*: I do think we should take our hats off to Mr Creed, the art academics and maybe the marketing gurus who assisted him in obtaining the arguably now demeaned *'Turner Prize'* for successfully exhibiting something so mundane...Turner must be turning in his grave!   Who would ever imagined it; only the art world could believe their own bollockese so much they would award such an eminently named prize to the creator, sorry not the creator, but the erector of such simplistic everyday items. So yes… I suppose somewhere along the line someone did possess some imagination. Not so much in the creation of the piece, but certainly in the composition of the supporting bollockese.

Does the above creations of Mr Creed require skill or some technical ability?
This, there is no problem with… My greatest respect goes out to *Alessandro Volta, Thomas Edison* and of course *budget-blinds.com.* Their technical ability is second to none. However, with regard to the skill and/or technical ability of Mr Creed relative to these pieces, well actually.. it's all been done before.

I suppose someone had to press the on and off switch! Or maybe he got some numpty to operate the exhibit for him.. like his work *No.2339*:

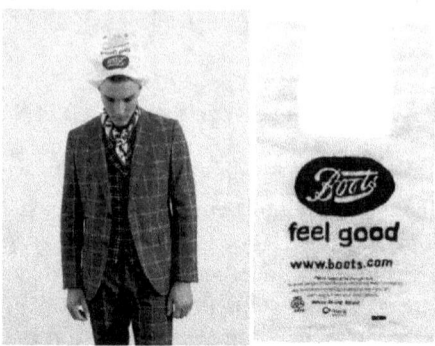

Martin Creed - Work No. 2339 (2015)

Does the piece portray something of beauty or express feelings / ideas of importance? It has to be said.. you can't see any beauty, in anything, if the lights are out. Nevertheless, they do come on every 30 seconds, so then of course if there is some beauty there you could see it. However, the problem with this piece is; the installation is set up in a blank room, so it's therefore reasonable to assume any beauty may be lacking. Ahh..but you could be standing next to someone or something that is. But this of course can't be guaranteed.

Okay…That brings us onto exploring if the pieces express any *feelings or ideas of importance*…Mr Creed and those art boffs championing his corner, suggest the darkness when the lights are off, portray feelings of *"..sadness & rain"*, while when the lights come on, we the masses, *"..feel happy and filled with sunshine"*. This seems all a bit weird… especially the rain analogy, and arguably pointless. Although it is generally accepted; us humans do prefer the light and do relate darkness to negative things like 'bogey men and death. Therefore, it's got to be said some of the bollockese analogy may be true-ish and the piece may influence the viewer's feelings as described. Nevertheless, however hard I've try to sort the 'wheat from the chuff' relative to the above bollockese, I struggle to find any ideas of importance being portrayed in any of Mr Creeds works…Although, I bet the bloke exhibiting Work *No. 2339* thinks the piece was important. But really, having now seen himself looking like a plonker, is kicking himself that he didn't pull the bag completely down over his face….Hang on a minute…I've just discovered the numpty in the bag is in fact Martin Creed himself…Thank god for that!

So is the piece '*Lights going on and off*' really Art? Not wanting anyone to think us so-called, "men in the street" are peeved in any way because we can't see the "cleverness" of Mr Creed....Well okay then let's be peeved and face it; the clever ones are the promoters of these works. Therefore taken on their own merit, this commentator reckons this installation of Mr Creed is seemingly nuts. The works just consist of recognisable every day functional items, but exhibited as Art. However, the question still remains; is it Art?

In the original form in which it was exhibited, it can be categorically stated; Mr Creed's '*lights going on and off*' falls short of being termed true Art. However, it does not require much more effort to make the piece Art inclusive.

All that is required is; a picture, may-be by *William Russell Flint* or *John Constable* or even by *Mr Turner* himself, hung on the blank wall for all to see when the lights do eventually come on...now that would be clever! Nevertheless, once again art bollockese has been successfully employed to promote such pieces and afford the creator, sorry erector, of this nonsense, high standing in the art-world establishment. This just begs one question...Why?   And the answer as screamed by Pink Floyd's '*Dark Side of the Moon*' must be; "Money". To conclude with a visual summing up of Mr Creed's work lets see his film of a "..*penis tumescing and detumesching*" ...on second thoughts, lets not.

Joe's Quote of Note for Mr Creed and his oddities: "Crazy is as crazy does,"... "*Mama always said you can't outgrow crazy.*" **Forrest Gump** *(attributed)*

CHAPTER 4

PAUL McCARTHY

McCarthy was born in Salt Lake City, Utah in 1945. He studied art at Weber State University in Ogden, Utah, and later continued to study at the University of Utah until 1969. He went on to study at the San Francisco Art Institute receiving a BFA in painting. In 1972 he studied film, video, and art at the University of Southern California receiving an MFA. From 1982 to 2002 he taught performance, video, installation, and performance art history at the University of California, Los Angeles. McCarthy currently works mainly in video and sculpture.

During the summer of 2008, Paul McCarthy's inflatable "Complex Shit", installed on the grounds of the *Paul Klee Centre* in Bern, Switzerland, took off in a wind, bringing down a power line, breaking a greenhouse window and a window at a children's home. This incident was widely reported internationally via news outlets in several languages with headlines like "Huge turd catastrophe for museum" and "Up in the sky: is it a turd or a plane?   *Source Wikipedia.*

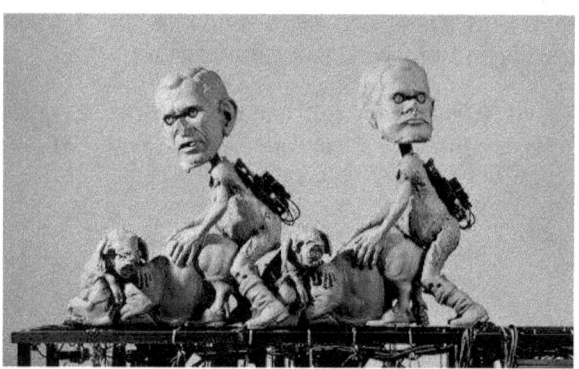

Images@ Paul McCarthy & Hauser & Wirth

Paul McCarthy - Train, Mechanical (2003-2009)
Steel, platinum silicone, fiberglass, rope, electrical and mechanical components
276.9 x 152.4 x 566.4 cm / 109 x 60 x 223 in

EXAMPLES of ART-BOLLOCKESE*:-

Comments from 'Art Experts' re. The Work's of PAUL McCARTHY:

Article from The Guardian UK Newspaper - Thursday 17 November 2011:

" Reader alert: the following is unpleasant. An identical pair of anamatronic sculptures of George W Bush are having anal sex with pigs in Hauser & Wirth's Savile Row gallery. The pigs are also gamely porking one another to riotous sound-effect squeals and the motorised wheeze of servo-powered pistons. The sculptures are beginning to look a teensy bit flayed. As you approach, the twin Bush sculptures swivel their heads and give you a Terminator stare, their pink silicon bodies still humping away. ..

...Going beyond taste is part of McCarthy's schtick. But whose eyes water now at the sight of McCarthy's giant butt-plugs, or the huge pendulous pair of testicles that dangle from a rickety wooden gibbet? They are mere incidents in a huge and inane raft of abused art materials and abandoned forms. McCarthy is nothing if not copious.

McCarthy himself, or rather his hairy, life-sized body-cast doppelgänger, is enthroned in Hauser & Wirth's Piccadilly gallery, in front of rows of empty church pews. Pot-bellied and naked, he is a mute and impotent king, cable-tied to his chair and surrounded with painting supplies. This is the artist as fallen hero, sage and fool....

...Once, in his hilarious and savage video Painter, McCarthy played a whining and infantile abstract expressionist, an overgrown baby dabbling in paint and screaming for money. Now he is both elevated and debased, sitting it out on a wooden stage. Down in the gallery's basement, there's a video running in which an assistant is having a go at the artist's replica with an electric carving-knife. Parody and mock yourself this much and you save the critic the job of complaint...

---

* **BOLLOCKESE** - Nonsensical verbiage or high-brow language used to communicate; unproven or biased opinion or an exaggerated truth; by a person who possesses or has pretensions of superior learning to project or promote items or concepts.

...This show often feels stretched, pumped-up and routine rather than genuinely violent and atavistic, the qualities I always liked in McCarthy's horrible and sometimes frightening world. Where do you go when you've already gone too far? McCarthy's self-portrait as king might well be a comment on his own artistic fate, and for that reason is the best thing here. Where once his art looked dangerous and subversive, rumbustious and bracingly obscene, his ever more strident antics now look tired, their bite gummy. This, more often than not, is the fate of an art of shocks. We get inured to it, as does its maker. What might become of the artist in late lyrical mode, when he gets beyond the pigs and the drool, the daily hump and grind of the big-career artist? Maybe McCarthy will sleep through it all, like the king in his dotage..."

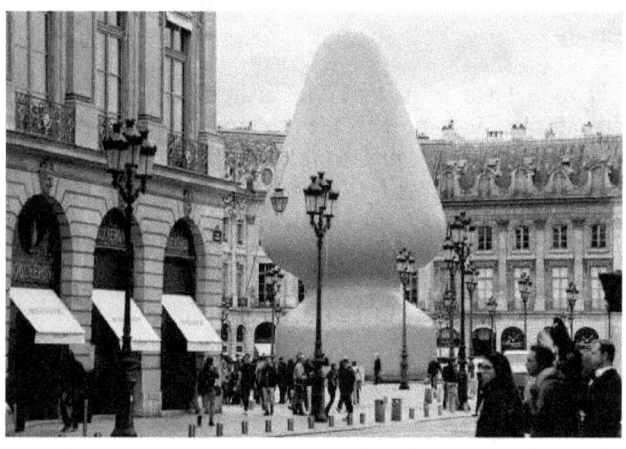

Hauser & Wirth @HauserWirth · 3h
Paul McCarthy's 'Tree' is now on display in Place Vendôme, Paris, as part of @FIAC 2014! #art #sculpture #paris
↩ Reply ⇄ Retweet ★ Favorite

Article by Art Critic; Cat Weaver - "How To Talk About Paul McCarthy"
October 22, 2014 :

" What, I ask you, should one expect if one asks artist Paul McCarthy to create a Christmas tree for the place of honour at a renowned, must-attend art fair? Well, it's Paul McCarthy, so there are only two possible outcomes: a turd or a butt plug.

This year, Paris got a butt plug. A — sah-weeeeet! — whopping, elegantly unembellished, minty green butt plug! Nicer than that gaudy, decked out whore of a tree that New York City erects at Rockefeller Center every year. Even, I'd say, in better taste.

"Of course this work is controversial," said Foire Internationale d'Art Contemporain (FIAC) director Jennifer Flay, "it plays on the ambiguity between a Christmas tree and a plug: this is neither a surprise nor a secret."

But despite his predictability and rather tasteful, understated delivery, the art world's most reliably scatological artist managed to shock people with his contribution to FIAC's "Hors les Murs" (or "Outside the Walls") sector.

How did that happen?

In July, a.. preview of McCarthy's *Chocolate Factory*, which would, in October, fill the newly renovated Monnaie de Paris with a giant solo show, and grace Paris's Place Vendôme with a giant inflatable "Christmas tree."

The ...story described a "wonderland experience" that "lures" visitors into a "fairytale forest of giant inflatable Christmas trees."

Without cracking a smile, the article went on to describe an *Eyes Wide Shut* sort of experience whereby one is drawn by curiosity into a tunnel of increasingly freaky rooms. First "we find a team of confectioners hard at work in a life-size, fully functioning chocolate factory," and, if we elect to go on after gorging on sweet brown confections, we open doors in a labyrinth of experiences and "a place of endless possibilities" where "reality gives way to the absurd.".... an image of a chocolate Santa holding a huge butt plug.

Towering at almost 25 meters on the Place Vendôme is Paul McCarthy's "Tree," a site specific sculpture conceived in relation to his concurrent exhibition *Chocolate Factory* at the Monnaie de Paris, his first major solo exhibition in Paris. A reference to both modernist sculpture and the iconic Christmas tree of western culture, McCarthy's sculpture stands proudly to celebrate his presence finally in Paris and alludes to the chocolate figurines his factory produces.

True, sometimes a giant sex toy is just a giant sex toy, but sometimes it is — take it from the artist himself — "more of an abstraction":

It all started with a joke: Originally I thought that the anal plug was shaped like a Brancusi sculpture. Then I thought that it resembled a Christmas tree. But it's an abstract work. People who find it offensive call it a plug, but for me it's more of an abstraction..."

Article by William S. Smith for 'Art in America' re. Paul McCarthy Installation 'WS' - McCarthy's interpretation of Disney's *Snow White. (02.10.2013)*:

" Even when his work has these carnal overtones, McCarthy is far from the "body artist" he was once billed as. There is an important difference between chocolate syrup and excrement, and McCarthy is concerned primarily with the associative play that happens when his cast is drenched in the former.

WS offered a rich, if repulsive, vision of sentimental America through the language of costumes, masks, makeup and set design. In this sense, *WS* belongs to a tradition of "world making," to borrow a concept from art historian Alex Potts, that includes Edward Kienholz's brothel nightmare *Roxy's* (1961-62) and Mike Kelley's high school musical *Day Is Done* (2005-06). Despite its detailed production design, *WS* staged a blunt collision between base materials and cherished abstractions. In a simple reversal (reflected in the logic of the protagonist's name), Disney's sanitized allegories of purity and youth were confronted with the brute realism of a dirty old man with a high-definition video camera.

This may be a "subversion" of an American icon, as the Armory's curators maintained, but who really has a stake in the sanctity of Disney's myths? Certainly no one over 17. As a figure of cultural oppression, Disney is a vague straw man who has been "subverted" to death already, most successfully in the subtle, unhinged work of Llynn Foulkes, Los Angeles' premier artist of Mickey Mouse paranoia.

If *WS* felt like an exhausted, vague parody of the culture industry, it found more traction as biography. Between McCarthy's lecherous father-figure act and the reconstruction of his childhood home, *WS* came across as an oddly personal tale, told through a common pop vocabulary. (Considering that McCarthy frequently collaborates with his son, Damon, *WS* may also be one of the all-time creepiest instances of father-son bonding.)

The scale of *WS* was a testament to the art world's current capacity for production value, which appears to be catching up to that of the entertainment industry McCarthy's work was meant to critique. *WS* was the centerpiece of what one publicist aptly dubbed "McCarthy Spring," an event that also included three related exhibitions at Hauser & Wirth's two Manhattan locations.

"Rebel Dabble Babble," a stripped-down, sexed-up take on *Rebel Without a Cause*, was presented in Chelsea, and a suite of nude "body casts" of McCarthy and Elyse Poppers, the White Snow actress, were on view uptown. (Another exhibition in Chelsea held in May featured tepid, luxurious wood sculptures depicting cherubic princes and princesses.)

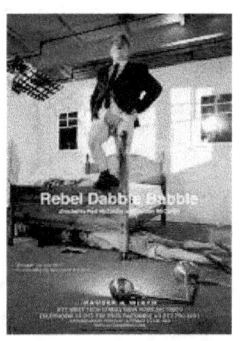

The ethics of McCarthy's work depends on his own participation in the debased carnival. In his videos McCarthy always takes on the most extreme humiliation himself. Yet this democratic approach to abjection belies an economic reality: the man playing an impotent fool and cavorting with nubile young women is, in fact, the CEO of a booming art industry. If McCarthy helped usher in a generation of post-studio artists in Southern California, he may also be at the crest of a new kind of studio system centered on a handful of powerful galleries and art stars. The import of *WS* lies not in another artist mining the movies for campy, transgressive imagery but in his indicating a new stratum of blockbuster high culture: the art world's version of Hollywood..."

 JOE C.THREWITT re. The Work's of PAUL McCARTHY:

Don't you just love how even the weirdest and pervie of pieces can be transformed into deep meaningful artworks with the skilful use of bollockese. Even the clever employment of negative bollockese has been used here to promote interest. This is because it has to be accepted, sex and nudity has always featured strongly in Art, including making many seriously deviant works socially acceptable. So let's say for Mr McCarthy sake; we accept his pieces can be recognised as Art. Nevertheless, what begs the question here is; without his academic and arty associates spewing bollockese, particularly about works due for exhibition; would his pieces stand up as 'quality art'? Which of course is what Joe Public is being influenced to believe here.

Well…this commentator thinks it should seem pretty clear to most reasonable people; Mr McCarthy is surely driven by some sort of manic sex craving. The chap like many of his ilk, appear obsessed with sex and seemingly the more deviant the better. Nevertheless, what is amazing is how the art world has managed to influence the majority of modern galleries to exhibit works that have been produced most likely as a pandering therapy for the likes of Mr McCarthy's ardent followers, whom some would argue have sex addictions beyond taking 'viagra'. Although as a positive thought; without being able to satisfy their obsessive sex syndromes by visiting Mr McCarthy's exhibitions, such individuals would probably be at home, eyes fixed to their Macs while wearing their dirty ones, watching pornography and pulling their pud all day.

However, as previously advocated, let us take the works as they appear without the bollockese. Some are definitely amusing in a toilet jokey kind of way. However, others pieces of McCarthy's, which are not included here, are extreme, to say the least. And because the more extreme depictions are not portrayed by actual humans, but images and puppetry, it seems he can convey hard core perverted porn to all un-sundry without being arrested by Miami-Vice's Detective Crockett and made to sign a sex register until death. It's also canny how Mr McCarthy can demean even USA presidents without legal recourse. The answer of course is parody.. and long may it reign!

What about the imagery and element of skill involved in the production of McCarthy pieces? As with most of the contemporary weirdy art set, the imagery always looks like it has been created by a child. It now seems most people accept new art will predominantly be like this, and although people turn up and gawp at these images, unless they read the constructed bollockese narrative, they haven't a scooby-doo what they are about. You don't have to believe me. Next time you're at a modern gallery, take time out to look at other visitors you will see many just look at these odd works, go Hmmm, and pass them by. This can be clearly seen with Mr McCarthy's giant *'Butt Plug / Christmas Tree'*. Generally people passing the apparition just see a green blob possibly a tree shaped green blob. And, as the photo shows, ignore it for what it is; another piece of new art dumped in the middle of a public space. Most have no idea it is meant to be a big 'Butt Plug', even if they have a camera drone to hand. Then why should they, unless they are also constantly on the deviant sex wavelength. Probably, if you could be bothered to ask, most would say, "It looks like a jolly green giant or a giant green chess piece that is blocking the bloody way out".

Okay let's look for something positive in these works by Mr McCarthy. Well it has to be accepted there has to be some technical skill in producing his pervie puppets and their electronic workings. Whether it is the recreation of the thrusting motion when engaging in rumpy-pumpy or something similar ..or even reproducing the 'squealing like a piggy' sounds. So yes it should be accepted; some element of skill is probably present here.

But is this really the 'quality art' the exponents of bollockese are telling us? Not forgetting this bollockese also paves the way for the art elite to decide what to exhibit in their exclusive galleries around the globe.

I'm afraid in the end this all comes down to us humans lust for sex and craving to view something shocking. Even, if we do find it distasteful and/or disturbing. Of course, it is accepted, human beings can get up to all sorts of debauchery. But, it's usually done in private. So, bring on the intellectual bollockese. Resultantly, by giving Mr McCarthy's pervie works some deep sociological meaning; we can all get to see pornography under the banner of it being 'Art'.

Basically, if you can label it as 'Art' and not pornography, which actually it is, but it isn't in the eyes of the law if its 'Art'...And even better when you are being told it's cool to view it.... Slam Dunk...Sold to the man and woman in the street.

It can therefore be agreed; sex depictions are always likely to be considered Art.. as we.. that's the royal we.. will always want to see, or at least sneak a look, at something most consider a private act. Yes...we are all voyeurs to a point, because it is human nature. Nevertheless, for most people there's no way you could be honest and come clean about this in accepted society. Instead we are fed academic bollockese about 'abstractism' and 'visions of sentimentalism'. And it is with these bollockese terms, the art intellectuals have convinced the law makers that Mr McCarthy, and his ilk, which there are an increasing amount, are quality artists. Therefore their 'Art', albeit really pornography, should be made available for public viewing.. and weirdly.. to be appreciated.

This acceptance of pornography as 'Art', into the public domain has achieved a couple of things. Primarily; to the art exhibitors it enables them to show something that people will always want to see. Even if it disgusts them.. because they have provided an academic reason why they can. That not only eleviates social embarrassment but more importantly means... chhh-ting, lots of dosh...even though 95% of people, if asked; would probably say how repulsive it is, because they feel they have to.

The other 5% are probably the weirdy artists who also are hoping to show off their therapeutic works and accordingly are happy to re-spout the bollockese they've been fed.

So summing up…and yes I know what you're thinking; Joe C. Threwitt will have to accept art bollockese has won the day for the masses, by enabling him to see hard core porn in a socially acceptable environment, rather than paying 'Erotica XXX.com' for the private privilege.

Ha...but consider this; maybe Joe Public is not so gullible…maybe he does recognise the bollockese being spouted for what it is…abstractism tosh. But, chooses to let it wash over him (as with the people passing the big green butt plug) because by accepting this is Art means we can all look at porn without becoming a Scotland Yard suspect for 'Operation Saddo'. Then once viewed, with any voyeuristic tendencies satisfied, you can walk away, call the artist a 'dirty perv '… and still seem cool to your partner… whom you hope in the mean time, has picked up a few ideas for later.

Joe's Quote of Note for Mr McCarthy and his crudities "…*You cant put a flower in a asshole and call it a vase*" **Adam Dark** (attributed)

CHAPTER 5

RACHEL WHITEREAD

C BE (born 20 April 1963) Rachel Whiteread is an English artist who primarily produces sculptures, which typically take the form of casts. She was the first woman to win the annual Turner Prize in 1993.

Many of Whiteread's works are casts of ordinary domestic objects and, in numerous cases, their so-called negative space. For example, she is known for making solid casts of the open space in and around pieces of furniture such as tables and chairs, architectural details and even entire rooms and buildings. She says the casts carry "the residue of years and years of use". Whiteread mainly focuses on the line and the form for her pieces.

While still at the Slade School of Art, Whiteread cast domestic objects and created her first sculpture, *Closet*. She made a plaster cast of the interior of a wooden wardrobe and covered it with black felt. It was based on comforting childhood memories of hiding in a dark closet. After she graduated she rented space for a studio using the Enterprise Allowance Scheme. She created *Shallow Breath* (1988), the cast of the underside of a bed, made not long after her father died. Both sculptures were exhibited in her first solo show in 1988 along with casts of other domestic pieces. The work all sold and allowed her to apply for grants to find funding for larger sculptures. *Source Wikipedia*

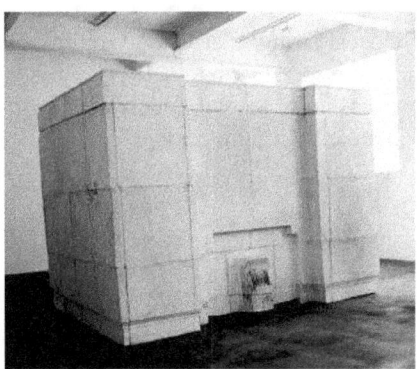

Image@ hamer.veto.udu

Rachel Whiteread – Ghost (1990)
London Stone

EXAMPLES of ART-BOLLOCKESE*:-

Comments from 'Art Experts' re. The Work's of RACHEL WHITEREAD:

Article by Art Writer Jonathan Jones; – "Rachel Whiteread is Britain's greatest living artist":

I just want to take a moment to salute Britain's greatest living artist. A few weeks ago I was in an American art museum looking at the modern masters. Pablo Picasso and Richard Serra share space with Sol LeWitt and Jackson Pollock in the tremendous collections of the National Gallery of Art in Washington DC. But not far from Barnett Newman's Stations of the Cross paintings, an unexpected thing from home caught my eye.

It was like seeing a ghost. In fact, I was seeing 'Ghost' – a sculpture by Rachel Whiteread that I first encountered, what, 20 years ago, in the London whose Dickensian chill it reproduces. Ghost is a cast of an entire room in an old-fashioned, perhaps Victorian, house. It is the solid trace of all the air that a room once contained. Empty space has become solid. Because it is solid, it is closed. Nothing can get in or out. On this side of the white surfaces of the massive block, engraved with negative images of fireplace, door, window and light switch, we wonder at the dark invisible silence within. Vanished lives, lost voices, forgotten loves are trapped in that fossilised room like prehistoric creatures in limestone.

Ghost is the closest living relative of Whiteread's destroyed artistic masterpiece 'House'. She made Ghost in 1990; three years later she took the same casting process to its logical conclusion by preserving the inner world of a house scheduled for demolition.

---

* **BOLLOCKESE** - Nonsensical verbiage or high-brow language used to communicate; unproven or biased opinion or an exaggerated truth; by a person who possesses or has pretensions of superior learning to project or promote items or concepts.

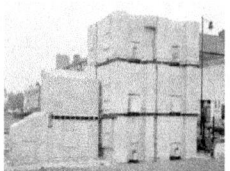

Photo by Sue Omerod

Rachel Whiteread – 'House'(1993)

The subsequent destruction of Whiteread's House by an unsympathetic council did immense harm to British art. Amid all the sound and fury that young British artists generated in the 90s – often signifying nothing – House was the real thing: a modern masterpiece.

And Whiteread herself is the real thing, a first-rank artist, as I realised with a new clarity in Washington. It goes to show why it is sometimes foolish to want to "save" British art for British collections. If all British art was in Britain, how would it become known internationally? In the absence of House, Whiteread's Ghost is the single most important British sculpture of our times – but I am delighted it is in one of America's best galleries. Here, among some of the key works of the modern age, you can truly assess Whiteread's achievement. It is one of the most powerful things in the museum. Whiteread is abstract, serious and profound. She is the modern British artist who matters.

Article by Art Writer Damon Hyldreth; – "Uncanny":

" ..Nineteenth-century sculptors referred to the process of bronze casting as life, death, and resurrection as the original live object was destroyed in the casting process and resurrected in bronze. In a similar but distinctly different manner Rachel Whiteread casts the space inside, around, and adjacent to objects that have been part of people's lives. This process and her choice of materials transform the residue of everyday life into ghostlike, uncanny spirit images of everyday objects.

Rather than using the traditional casting process of making molds of objects and then casting them in a different material, Whiteread uses the objects themselves as molds. For example her 2002 sculpture "Sequel IV", is a casting of the enclosing space surrounding the backs of a library shelf done in plaster. This is a reversal of a bookshelf as the titles are hidden and the books inaccessible. Instead of inviting browsing, these books are inaccessible shadows, frozen in time, reflecting hidden knowledge. It is as if we came upon an ancient ruin of a library.

Whiteread creates objects that are redolent of a mirror world of strange traces of human life, the ghosts of our common existence. These negative sculptures of domesticity, records of the traces of people's lives "seem to emphasize the fact that the objects they represent are not themselves there, and critics have often regarded her work to be redolent of death and absence. " This is reference to death and absence is evident in her 1990 "Ether" and her 1996 "Untitled (Orange Bath)" which are castings of the enclosing space surrounding and supporting Victorian bathtubs. The tubs and their enclosures served as the molds for the plaster and organic orange colored rubber and polystyrene castings. "Ether " which closely resembles a stone Greek sarcophagus is "a coffin like form, which, in turn, alludes to the practice of casting death masks." "Orange Bath " reverses this affect by resembling a sarcophagus made of petrified orange jello.

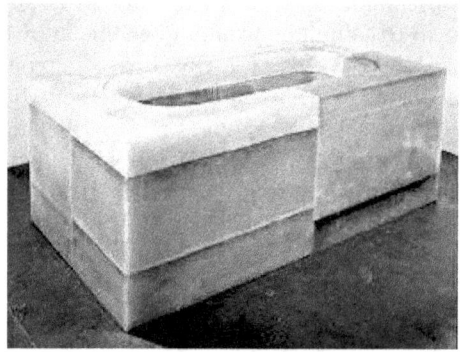

Image @www.artnet.com

Rachel Whiteread – 'Orange Bath'

Whiteread's doubles of the discarded objects of our lives have an uncanny ghostlike presence. Sigmund Freud discussed this affect in his essay: *The Uncanny*. Freud postulated that "the 'double' was originally an insurance against the destruction of the ego, an 'energetic denial of the power of death', ... and probably the 'immortal' soul was the first 'double' of the body..."

In today's society, as in times past, people collect and surround themselves with objects and elements that bring a homelike comfort to their daily lives. These objects, an outer manifestation of the ego, create an outer protective shell to our lives. However when we outgrow these objects and discard them as old dead things, their ego supporting function reverses itself, and "the 'double' reverses its aspect. From having been an assurance of immortality, it becomes the uncanny harbinger of death."

The power of Rachel Whiteread's sculptures stem from its unconscious connection to our repressed fear of death in that they are the ghostlike manifestations of the hidden, discarded elements of our lives. Freud mirrors this observation defining the uncanny as "in reality nothing new or alien, but something which is familiar and old established in the mind and which has become alienated from it only through the process of repression."

Thought and experience are not the only things that sanction human values. The values that belong to daydreaming mark humanity in its depths. Daydreaming even has a privilege of auto valorization. It derives direct pleasure from its own being. Therefore, the places in which we have experienced daydreaming reconstitute themselves in a new daydream, and it is because our memories of former dwelling -places are relived as daydreams that these dwelling places of the past remain in us for all time.

Thus the places and objects of our lives constitute the material for our dreams and Whiteread manifests in her work the dreamlike traces of our memories of place, what is invisible becomes visible, what is inside become the outside of her sculptures....

.... The brick and wood structure of the house was used as a mold for the casting of "House". After the structure was stripped away, what was left was a ghostlike monument to the private insides of a dwelling turned inside out.

It set a familiar past in the space-time of today; it made present something which was absent; it was the space of a house no longer there. Secondly, however, it worked spatially: it turned the space inside out. The private was open to public view....the intimate was made monumental and yet retained its intimacy.

This was a reversal of an enclosing, comforting, dwelling, a place of repose and comfort, a symbol of domestic hopes and dreams. What was left was a monument to one's most private moments but with the privacy stripped bare and petrified. "House" monumentalized the past in a subversive manner, instead of allowing for a connection to and retrieval of the past, "House" subverted the warm cozy memories of home. According to Doreen Massey, *House* triggered a sense of nostalgia in the public arena because it disrupted the time and space of the present. As a site of memory that revolved around collective heritage, *House* was inaccessible and therefore did not allow retrieval of the past. In this respect, the cast was uncomfortably subversive. Traditionally at a site of memory buildings are retained and nostalgia is very often commodified…Narrative features of the life of 193 Grove Road were interred in concrete as *House* became a monument to memory; a souvenir of daydreams inscribed with the cultural significance.

Someone once called Whiteread's work "Minimalism with a heart". Minimalism was for the most part a cold and geometric reaction against the self-expression of the feelings, which was a part of abstract expressionism. In contrast, Whiteread's work is geometry softened and incorporates the feelings of memory of place. Whereas Minimalism practiced a sense of detachment and reduction to pure, self-referential form, Whiteread's sculptures affirm their connection to the world of objects and space…."

***Extract from an Article by Art Writer; Nicholas Wroe - "Rachel Whiteread - A Life in Art"** Saturday 6 April 2013* :

" It is almost exactly 20 years since Rachel Whiteread received official approval from a fractious coalition of councillors and residents in east London to create what still remains her best-known artwork, *House*. By the spring of 1993 there had already been two years of preparation for the project. Work eventually began that summer on the last remaining property in a demolished terrace on Grove Road, Bow.

Liquid concrete – the same product that is used to patch up the white cliffs of Dover – was sprayed on to the house's interior to create a cast, and then the external walls were carefully removed. The work was finally finished in late autumn, revealing a full-sized, inverse representation of the three-storey home, complete with outlines of fireplaces, windows, architraves and staircases. Less than a month after its official opening, Whiteread, aged just 30, was awarded the Turner prize.
The work was Whiteread's most ambitious exploration to date of the utterly familiar, yet almost entirely overlooked. And within the apparently blank concrete surface were exposed the affecting remnants of lives lived. Whiteread found herself being thanked by two former residents of the demolished terrace for "making their memories real". "People still talk to me a lot about *House*," she says today. "It still seems to be incredibly evocative and people can bring it up in their mind's eye.

That's obviously very pleasing, but I also know that part of it is undoubtedly to do with the way it was destroyed."

For all the praise *House* attracted, it was also a lightning conductor for varying degrees of opportunistic political and artistic objection. Unofficial laureate of east London Iain Sinclair captured well the "freakish alliance of extremes" that eventually coalesced in opposition: "Come in the K Foundation, Brian Sewell, Stewart Home, Councillor Eric Flounders. Come in Class War, the BNP, and the M11 protest lobby." On the very day of the Turner prize announcement, a sub-committee of the local authority made the decision that the lease should not be renewed, and so in January 1994, less than four months after its completion, *House* was demolished….."

JOE C.THREWITT re. The Work's of RACHEL WHITEREAD:

The first thing to pick up on with Ms Whiteread is, how the hell did she get planning permission to dump her concrete in the middle of a green field?

One feels she achieved the placement of these early works of 'inside-out moulds of buildings', because the respective councils needed something for local graffiti chavs to draw on. But some important questions beg to be answered here. Why would anyone want to make a cast of such structures? And then.. having decided this may be a fun thing to do… Who in their right mind would encourage it, let alone acquiesce or sponsor such a thing? It does therefore make a reasonable person wonder if anyone on the council planning committee failed in their duty to disclose a conflict of interest, or at least failed to canvas their local community properly.

What does seem clear is; Ms Whiteread must have recruited sponsors brilliant at bollockese to ensure some income would be forthcoming from this wild idea before any cement was sprayed. This must be the case, as anyone who has just had their drive done will agree…cement ain't cheap…definitely the amount needed for Ms Whiteread's fun filled endeavours.

However, lets now begin considering if the pieces described are true Art?

With regard to; imagination and skill in execution; Ms Whiteread certainly seems to have one hell of an imagination, weird but definitely imaginative. And the skill required to get all that concrete into those crevices and corners is undoubtedly truly amazing. Not forgetting once the concrete has set.. getting it out of its mould...and then transferring it to where its to be exhibited. A logistical marvel! But is the finished article *a thing of beauty or something of importance*?

The man or lady on the omnibus will always accept, as already mentioned; 'beauty is in the eye of the beholder'. But, hang on a minute; how many beholders does it make to be certain something really holds beauty? Does it take one, a couple, or say ten? This of course is the key if you are going to place your work in the middle of a public space. What also seems clear in the art world, and these pieces seem prime examples, is if there's a slightest chance anyone somewhere thinks something created can be liked, visually or otherwise.. spin the bollockese.. and bingo we have a piece of Art.

Therefore to assess Ms Whiteread work on this basis; she herself, probably thinks her creations look good, as too would the person who used the toilet she has cast. So that is at least two. This is not withstanding all those who can make money out of her fun packed idea. This would include artwork marketing managers, gallery owners in on the jolly-jape and all the interested individuals supplying the equipment and expertise to make and exhibit her pieces. Therefore, all these people will certainly profess that such a chunk of concrete is something of beauty to them. This we have to accept...unless we could forcibly connect them up to a lie-detector. Hey there's an idea! We could then invite people to witness it and then sell it as an art installation. Damn..I think its already been done!

The winner here for Ms Whiteread, is that the bollockese brigade have championed her concept as Art portraying something of historical importance. Even Sigmund Freud, the grand master of bollockese has had one of his essays high-jacked in support of Ms Whiteread artworks. It being claimed, the casts made of buildings and other items of bygone times have profound meaning. It has been spouted by individuals promoting Ms Whiteread, that her works are records of importance of how the, *"..not so well heeled"* use to live. So there you have it. That concrete apparition in your local field could at a push be termed a piece of Art.

Art it maybe, but surely it has to be seen as a piece of self-indulgent nonsense. Any person in control of their faculties and without any of the personal interests mentioned, would scream 'blue murder' if it were plonked outside their 'des-res' or village green. Just imagine it; your lovely English village green in all its splendour with one of Ms Whiteread's chunks of concrete bang in the middle!

These works of Ms Whiteread, again beg the question; why are the creators of such nonsense's allowed to be held in such high esteem? The truth seemingly is; they are completely reliant on the bollockese to create a narrative of reason to explain exactly what it is you're looking at. Therefore to any reasonable person viewing such works without any explanation, would they find them likable to the eye? It seems most unlikely to this commentator and I would suggest without much argument, to the majority of the populous. We are told the concrete 'House' has, "..subverted the warm cosy memories of home"...and triggered, "a sense of nostalgia in the public arena because it disrupted the time and space of the present." Sorry matey, these are just eye-sores with Joe Public being taken for the block-heads they must be if they believe any of the unadulterated bollockese accompanying these concrete b..locks depicting your old-mums fireplace.

As for saluting Britain's greatest living artist. I think the salute should really go to the cement company 'Blue Circle' ...although weren't they bought out by the French not long ago?

Joe's Quote of Note for Ms Whiteread and her 'Inside Out' indulgencies:
"The problem with contemporary art is that no one bothers to do the research necessary to give people what they want." **Michael Scott**

CHAPTER 6

LUCIO FONTANA

Lucio Fontana was an Argentine-Italian artist known as the founder of Spatialism, an art movement that focused on the spatial qualities of sculpture and paintings with the goal of breaking through the two-dimensionality of the traditional picture plane.

He was best known for his monochrome canvases known as *Concetti Spaziali* that he would cut or puncture, leaving distinctive gaping slash marks and holes that imbued the finished work with an almost violent energy...Fontana had widespread impact on the following generation of artists, who began to use installation media more aggressively to address the dynamics of space in gallery environments and Land Art. Born on February 19, 1899 in Rosario de Santa Fé, Argentina, the painter and sculptor spent his career travelling between Argentina and Italy. Fontana died on September 7, 1968 in Varese, Italy at the age of 69, just two years after being awarded the Grand Prize for painting at the Venice Biennale.

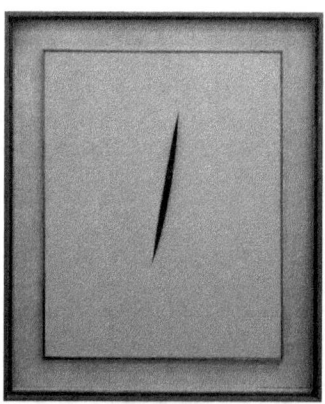

Image@Lucio Fondazione / Lucio Fontana, Milan.

Lucio Fontana - 'Waiting' (1960)
Concetto spaziale 'Attesa'
Purchase Price circa $1.5 Million

EXAMPLES of ART- BOLLOCKESE*:-

Comments from 'Art Experts' re. The Work's of LUCIO FONTANA:

Extract from an Article by Art Writer; Sophie Howarth - May 2000 for the Tate Website. :

" Fontana first began puncturing the surface of paper or canvas in the late 1940s, blurring the distinction between two and three dimensionality. Recognising the importance of this innovation, he continued, through the 1950s and 1960s, to seek different ways of developing the hole as his signature gesture. The first *Tagli* were made in the late summer and early autumn of 1958. They comprised small, often diagonal incisions, composed in groups over unprimed canvases. During 1959 these tentative slits evolved into single, more decisive slashes, as in the present work. Each cut was made with a single gesture using a sharp blade, and the canvases were then backed with strong black gauze giving the appearance of a void behind. In 1968 Fontana told an interviewer that, 'my discovery was the hole and that's it. I am happy to go to the grave after such a discovery' (quoted in Whitfield, p.12).

Fontana experimented with both the size and shape of the *Tagli* and painted a number of the canvases in bright monochrome colours. From the earliest works in the series, he wrote the word 'Attesa', meaning 'expectation' or 'hope', on the back of all the canvases with one cut, and 'Attese' (plural) on all those with multiple cuts. This added a temporal dimension to the generic title 'Spatial Concept', which he gave to all his works from the late 1940s. In 1966 Fontana presented an entire room of white *Tagli* at the Venice Biennale, claiming that he had found a way of 'giving the spectator an impression of spatial calm, of cosmic rigour, of serenity in infinity' (Crispolti, p.38).

---

* **BOLLOCKESE** - Nonsensical verbiage or high-brow language used to communicate; unproven or biased opinion or an exaggerated truth; by a person who possesses or has pretensions of superior learning to project or promote items or concepts.

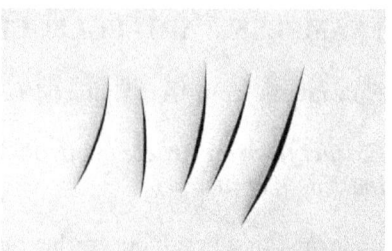

LUCIO FONTANA
Concetto spaziale, Attese
Purchased for circa £6 Million

Image@alaintruong.wordpress.com

In the instances where Fontana slashed an unpainted canvas, as in the present work, there is a particular affinity between the rawness of the surface and the primordial character of the gesture itself. Destruction and creation were bound together in these works. The same gesture that negated the canvas as a purely pictorial vehicle also opened up its sculptural possibilities. 'Art dies but is saved by gesture', Fontana wrote in 1948 (*Lucio Fontana 1899-1968: A Retrospective*, exhibition catalogue, Solomon R. Guggenheim Museum, New York 1977, p.19). Such rhetoric was characteristic of *Spazialismo*, the movement he founded in 1947 when he returned to Milan after spending the war years in Buenos Aires.

Many of Fontana's marks - slashes, gouges, puncturings - evoke pain, and in particular suggest wounds to the skin. His *Nature* series of sculptures…. clearly reference female genitalia and the *Tagli* can also be interpreted in this light…"

Extract from an Article by Art Writer; Anthony White - "No Form Can Be Spatial, The Origins of Lucio Fontana's Spatial Concept":

"….Fontana distanced his work from the conventions of late modernist easel painting by refusing a paradigm of artistic practice that was prevalent in Europe during the 1950s and 1960s – the gestural school of Informal painting. One of the leading painters of this movement, the French artist Georges Mathieu, was inspired by the Surrealist technique of automatic drawing, wherein the artist abdicates a degree of control by allowing the pencil or pen to roam freely over the page. Mathieu had utterly transformed this technique by turning it into a ritualised performance where he literally attacked the canvas with violent strokes of paint. The result was a kind of spectacular graffiti art in which the gesture became a sublime trace of the artist's presence, making the author the subject of the work.

Although the punctures in Fontana's *Spatial concept* demonstrate that an event of sheer physical impact has occurred, Fontana was completely averse to Informal painting and the types of psychological readings that were attached to it. 'I am not informal', he declared, the informal seeks the result in the gesture … my nature is attracted rather to space'. One cannot deny that Fontana's works are the result of a certain kind of action but they were not intended as records of his own physical or intellectual presence. As Fontana insisted, 'The artist must have the courage to stop idolizing himself, to stop seeing himself as the centre of the earth and of all things.

As evidence of this, the puncture technique in *Spatial concept* with its repetitive, machine-gunned appearance, does not allow for the kind of expressive effects common to gestural art. Rather, as contemporary viewers noted, this technique has more in common with the mechanical punches made in a tram-ticket. As Lawrence Alloway observed of an exhibition of earlier punctured paintings in 1957; 'like holes in a punched card, like bullet holes in a wall, the holes carry information'. Furthermore, the fact that the mark is a lack – an absence of canvas – in the pictorial field pointedly withdraws the artist's figure from the work in order to allow another dimension of painting to emerge…"

 JOE C.THREWITT re. The Work's of LUCIO FONTANA:

It has to be accepted; it's not good form to give the deceased a hard time, as they are unable to make any reasonable response, as of course would be their right. Nevertheless, it is felt some of the so-called contemporary artist's legacies involving works showing apparent little effort, should be re-examined as they undoubtedly formed part of the art-dumbing-down generation. This commentator like many I'm sure, believes Mr Fontana is one such artist. However, Lucio Fontana during an era of conservative thinking, managed to convince the art world he was a bit special, albeit his work was simplistic to say the least. It could be argued Mr Fontana could be considered one of the first to produce crazy art concepts. Nevertheless, unlike contemporary creators of nonsense art of today, there were fewer art intellectuals willing to put their 'old chap' on the block to champion works involving suspect creativity and skill, which lets face it we have here.

Probably much of Mr Fontana's success is down to his own salesmanship bollockese and contacts with like minded art-boffins of that era open to his influences. Think about it; with little or no support for your creations because they're (i) crazy or possess non-conforming concepts and (ii) so simple they would struggle to win a pre-school gold star…What can be done to make them credible and get them out there ? Answer…Invent an Art 'ism'.

It been done before to great success: Paul Durand-Ruel – Impression-ism (Late1800's); Roger Fry's canny marketing ploy for Manet - Post Impression-ism (late 1800's); Braque & Picasso's – Cub-ism (1910ish); Andre Breton – Surreal-ism (1924) and Art intellectual Robert Coates - Abstract Expression-ism (popularised version 1940's) when promoting his New York mates; Arshile Gorky, Jackson Pollock and Willem de Kooning.

It has been suggested (yep..by me; Joe C. Threwitt), as each art-ism has been introduced the skill in execution of artistic works has been eroded. If Mr Fontana's 'Spacial-ism' is anything to go by; the case appears proven! However, to be fair to these passed advocates of art-isms, it seems as much a consequence of modern marketing as anything. It seems pretty clear these artworks determined by 'isms' as a replacement for technical ability would not have come about if they were not accompanied by a myriad of art-intellectuals bollockese.

Nevertheless, it's reasonable to accept everybody wants to make a quick buck with little effort, and the art-world is no different. Therefore, to generate funds to accumulate faster wealth for both artist and their dealers, there is increasingly no time for pedantic excellence. This is born out by simply looking at what galleries have chosen to exhibit over recent years. In doing so it appears one way of achieving this is to make a particular art nonsense that can easily be produced appear special. As already mentioned, this is simply done by creating an 'ism' for it. This enables the creator to dumb down the skill…*which in-turn* enables the works to be knocked up easily thus more prolific… *which in-turn* increases income for both creators and sellers. This 'ism' marketing ploy is so obviously a piss-take of Joe Public and yet somehow because it emanates from the so called intellectuals… we buy in!

Come on JP its time to 'get a grip' and 'say what you see'! The constant here is; if it looks nonsense it is nonsense, and Stanley-knifing a canvas and marketing it for £Millions is an absolutely brilliant bit of marketing, equivalent of selling pebbles on a beach, but slicing a slit in a canvas is still incredulous nonsense.

Nevertheless, although accepting Mr Fontana's works may involve the required criteria to be termed Art, it is suggested without his and others intellectual bollockese interventions, for the reasons mentioned, it simply wouldn't pass muster. It is what it is; intellectually hyped simpleton art.

Mr Fontana's and his art intellectual supporters claims that Spatialism, is: *".. an art movement that focused on the spatial qualities of sculpture and paintings with the goal of breaking through the two-dimensionality of the traditional picture plane."* And even better, *"Art dies but is saved by gesture"*. And even better than that, Fontana's *"...slashes, gouges, puncturings - evoke pain, and in particular suggest wounds to the skin. His Nature series of sculptures.... clearly reference female genitalia and the Tagli (Cuts) can also be interpreted in this light."*

The art-bollockese merchants have definitely been busy here. They've used every trick in the book, including the old 'sex' chestnut to sale this concept. And yes, people have paid £Millions for these works with Mr Fontana going down in art history as a great art innovator.   To top his career, Mr Fontana was awarded the 1968 Grand Prize for painting at the Venice Biennale. Wow.. the judges must have spent sometime on the Grappa before awarding that one! So there you have it, Mr Fontana sits amongst Italy's finest; Michelangelo, Raphael, Botticelli, Titian and Da-Vinci. What do you mean I'm having a laugh...not me.. but the art bollockese bods definitely are, as they've managed to undermine the soul and brilliance of Italian Art in one foul swoop.

Joe's Quote of Note for Mr Fontana and his canvas incisions: *"Nonsense is the sixth sense that makes you disbelieve the other five."* **(non-attributed)**

CHAPTER 7

BARBARA KRUGER

B arbara Kruger is an American conceptual artist. Much of her work consists of black-and-white photographs overlaid with declarative captions—in white-on-red Futura Bold Oblique or Helvetica Ultra Condensed.

Born: January 26, 1945, Newark, New Jersey, United States

Education: Syracuse University, Weequahic High School, Parsons School of Design, School of Visual Arts.

At the beginning of her art career, she was intimidated to enter New York galleries due to the art scene which was an atmosphere that, to her, did not welcome "particularly independent, non-masochistic women." However, she received early support for her projects from groups such as the Public Art Fund that encouraged her to continue art making. She switched to her modern practice of collage in the early 80's. *Source Wikipedia.*

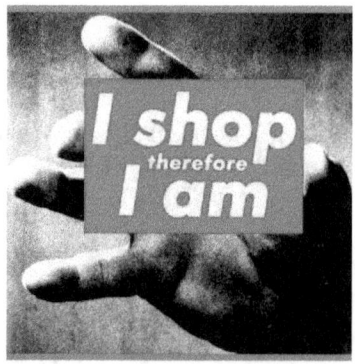

image Courtesy of Artist & Mary Boone Gallery.

Barbara Kruger - Untitled (I shop therefore I am) 1987
Size: 281.9 x 287 cm. (111 x 113 in.)
Genre: Abstract Art
Purchased for $600,000.

EXAMPLES of ART- BOLLOCKESE*:-

Comments from 'Art Experts' re. The Work's of BARBARA KRUGER:

Extract from article written for: www.noaozielart.weebly.com :

" Barbra Kruger's photograph gives representation to consumption in terms of the literal meaning of the word. By displaying the words, *"I Shop Therefore I Am,"* Kruger is making a statement in regards to material consumption. The open-ended statement allows the viewer to re-think materialism. Kruger challenges the notion of consumption. As well as this, she challenges the audience's perception. By doing this she offers two meanings in this artwork. The simplicity of the photograph, allows the audience to focus entirely on the statement that Kruger is making. As Kruger previously had a career in advertising, her knowledge allowed her to arrest the audiences attention. This resulted in her choice in colour, which attracts and demands the audiences attention. Barbra Kruger's artwork has stemmed from Descartes' philosophy of "I think therefore I am". She has appropriated this statement to fit the idea of material consumption, where Descartes' initial meaning had nothing to do with Kruger's intentions. The artwork was ironically printed onto thousands of shopping bags, t-shirts and other products of consumption…"

Extract from an Article written for the 'Smithsonian Magazine' July 2012 :

"….In addition to being a self-proclaimed "news junkie" and bookmarking the *Guardian* and other such serious sites, Kruger is a big student of reality shows, she told me. Which makes sense in a way: Her work is all about skewed representations of reality. How we pose as ourselves. She discoursed knowingly about current trends in reality shows, including the "preppers" (preparing for the apocalypse) and the storage wars and the hoarder shows. Those shows, she thinks, tell us important things about value, materialism and consumerism.

Kruger has immersed herself in such abstruse thinkers as Walter Benjamin, the prewar post-modernist ("Did you know he was a

---

* **BOLLOCKESE** - Nonsensical verbiage or high-brow language used to communicate; unproven or biased opinion or an exaggerated truth; by a person who possesses or has pretensions of superior learning to project or promote items or concepts.

compulsive shopper? Read his *Moscow Diary!*"), and Pierre Bourdieu, the influential postmodern French intellectual responsible for the concept of "cultural capital" (the idea that status, "prestige" and media recognition count as much as money when it comes to assessing power). But she knows theory is not enough. She needs to wade into the muddy river of American culture, panning for iconic words and images like a miner looking for gold in a fast-running stream, extracting the nuggets and giving them a setting and a polish so they can serve as our mirror.

Christopher Ricks, a former Oxford professor of poetry, once told me the simplest way to recognize value in art: It is "that which continues to repay attention." And Barbara Kruger's words not only repay but demand attention from us. Her work has become more relevant than ever at a time when we are inundated by words in a dizzying, delirious way— by the torrent, the tidal wave, the tsunami unleashed by the Internet. "What do you read, my lord?" Polonius asks Hamlet. "Words, words, words," he replies. Meaningless words. And that is what they threaten to become as we drown in oceans of text on the web. Pixels, pixels, pixels."

Article taken from The Independent (UK) Newspaper - Sunday 8 May 2011 :

" Barbara Kruger isn't just paying lip service to the working class in the manner of certain politically engaged artists of her generation.....
.....Her renown is tied in to the immediacy of her work, particularly the found black and white photography from mid-century magazines that she slathered with slogans in oblique Futura bold type, dealing with conformity, love, consumerism, the female condition, the problems of co-existence and more ("Think like us, Look like us"; "Your body is a battleground"; "Love for sale").

Her enduring proximity to popular culture – she still designs the odd magazine cover (most recently for W magazine in the US and Wallpaper in the UK), watches reality TV ("I see you have this British version of Jersey Shore that's something about Essex..."), and thrives on websites – perhaps explains why her work remains accessible and current....

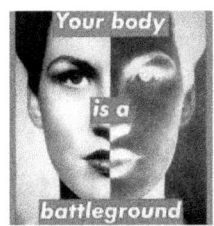

… She has printed her work on tote bags and billboards and created immersive videos since the early 1990s, working with multi-screens in architectural spaces because, she says, architecture is really her first love. The latest video installation – short scenes, played out on four huge screens, that include white male comics making light of human intolerance, depictions of the main world religions at their most ritualistic, and a smug director patronising his actress – questions everything from our relationship with technology to reality TV. Twice the viewer is plunged into darkness, captured in the space and unable to avoid a soliloquy of loss. The show is named after a quote by the post-colonialist critical theorist, Homi K Bhabha, now a professor at Harvard: "The globe shrinks for those that own it".

"I try to make work about how we are to one another," says Kruger. It is her mantra: you won't find an interview where she doesn't say this. …For her first major show in a British gallery in years, Kruger has assembled slews of exhortations, instructions, propositions, rejoinders and exclamations that appear with matching abruptness on the museum walls. They have the status of overheard speech, of shouts from the crowd or disembodied rhetoric, of urgings, rebukes, demands and counter-demands, and they work against each other all the time.

At best they may inspire thought, analysis, debate; at their worst they are hectoring banalities on the lowest level of phatic speech. "Hello Goodbye" runs one classically irritating play-off.

The enormous space of the main upstairs gallery is covered floor to lintel in capital letters 10 and even 20 feet high, in black, white and bright green that blaze and glare, leaving fierce after-images on the retina. "Be Here Now"; "Remember Me"; "Who Will Write The History of Tears?"; "The Brutal, Relentless, Fearful End of It All". (What does that mean, if it means anything at all? How can an end be relentless?)

The floor is covered with waves of words over which one must walk to make out the next, and the next. They accumulate into one long list – lovers, singers, speakers, posers, thinkers, feelers (Kruger likes a little rhythm and rhyme) – stretching away into the distance. Intellectuals, acolytes, sycophants and professors: can she be talking directly to Oxford?

Are these words random sneers (and if so, whose?); are they categories or labels? Do they have agency? Timothy Williamson, Wykeham professor of logic at the University of Oxford, has contributed a catalogue essay on the subject – words as labels, the nature of belief, the value of uncertainty, binary oppositions – and very fascinating it is too....

.... The walls bear questions to which there is only one right answer, one senses. "Is There Life Without Pain?" Well, perhaps you believe there is, perhaps that is your joyous experience. It's always hard to read the tone of Kruger's work – that is its essential and uppermost characteristic, in fact – but one can't help thinking she'd find that answer callow or complacent. For there's no doubt that she means to keep you on the alert, not relaxing into peaceful contemplation (is *what* all there is?) "You Are Not Yourself" (Go on then, who am I, and isn't this pretty basic ontology?) A flashing screen in the next gallery alternates names and images of consumer goods – including art, incidentally – before declaring (three times over) – Plenty Should Be Enough!"

Kruger is capable of eloquent concision. One of the works in this show is simply a sentence that builds to a portrait. "Thanks to yoga, yoghurt, life coaches, art, ashrams, philanthropy, real estate, pets, shopping and rehab, you've found peace." It's a miniature life. It is not, on the other hand, Dorothy Parker. Kruger is rarely as mordant as one might hope, given her lifelong survey of social culture, and nor is she quite the artist as anthropologist. The observation is all there, to be sure; a wall of emoticons opposite a wall of words gets to the nub of it. Why bother to examine what you feel, still less trouble to find the right words, when you can just use a dumb old smiley? Language loses the battle; the world shrinks even further.

Kruger presents a globe deafened by perpetual communication, in which everyone is online all the time, nobody is listening to anyone else, texting and tweeting are contracting not just language but thought. She was on to this long in advance. The problem, in a sense, is that her own work partakes of exactly this ruthless and simplifying brevity.

"I'm right and you're wrong". "Talk is cheap". "Fuck you". It's like having two kids in nonstop spat in the back of the car. And on the rare occasions when the disembodied voice or voices suddenly appear to be that of the artist herself – "Stop Texting" shouts the screen, alternating with dire photographs of car crashes – one almost misses the to and fro for the sense of receiving a public health warning…"

 JOE C.THREWITT re. The Work's of BARBARA KRUGER:

What's the first thing that comes into you head here? Yep.. you got it.. cutting and sticking in a teenagers scrapbook or even a 'Midsomer Murders' ransom note. What seems clear and becoming disturbingly consistent with these so called contemporary artists is; the skill level to produce their works is little more than zilch. Therefore, although you could probably knock one of these works up in a few hours, the art establishment has valued them at the equivalent of an average Joe's 25 year salary! It's no wonder everyone with little or no skill is having a crack.

However, what has also become very clear is; those who have succeeded, which there's no doubt Ms Kruger has, have had their works hyped with bollockese by art intellectuals and columnists. These bollockese exponents, for some reason or another have selected particular pieces of work from what appears to be random creative (*this word is used loosely*) individuals. In some instances, as with most careers in life, this may also be down to whom one knows in the art establishment…god forbid!

The need to draw your attention to this is because it seems hard to understand why, with so many brilliant poster manufacturers employing hundreds, if not thousands, of skilled technical illustrators, has Ms Kruger been singled out for stardom? There is no doubt her works hold some political or social message she is championing. And, there is no doubt she puts it across in a clever simplistic poster type way. But surely you have to ask yourself; what makes these works shine above all the other advertising billboard dross out there? Just take a walk along your local high street and view the plethora of images advertising some cause or product. Some of the advertising pieces hold as much impact as Ms Krugers works, with many requiring far more competence and skill in execution. So the question remains; why has Ms Kruger's images incorporating her feminist outcries proved so special and thus rewarding to her and of course her marketing supporters?

Bollockese of course…Unlike her fellow poster designers she has the ear of the 'art queen makers', namely; art intellectuals who can gush bollockese on her behalf. You have to be a chosen-one to exhibit at galleries like Larry Gagosians, as you do with many other well known galleries. It is accepted Ms Kruger has vast experience in putting her views across within her creations, but as good as they are, without the art intellectual bollockese support to go along with them, the images alone would probably be dismissed as just another socio-political rant.

Just taking the example of bollockese spouted by an art intellectual employed by a national newspaper seems to say it all:
"..Her renown is tied in to the immediacy of her work, particularly the found black and white photography from mid-century magazines that she slathered with slogans in oblique Futura bold type, dealing with conformity, love, consumerism, the female condition, the problems of co-existence and more ("Think like us, Look like us"; "Your body is a battleground"; "Love for sale").

There are many quality poster technical illustrators whom would love to have their work hyped in such a way. Many of whom it could be argued show greater skill and wit in their commercial creations. Nevertheless, they are destined to remain part of a skilled commercial work-force rather than have individual notoriety, because they lack the marketing bollockese acumen or intellectual art contacts now necessary for so called 'top gallery' recognition. This in itself is a good reason why; art should be seen for what it is and not what it's suppose to be. Then and only then will we return to having exceptional skill as an essential element of contemporary art creativity.

That's the soap box rant over.. it must be catching!

Joe's Quote of Note for Ms Kruger and her opinionated posters: *"There is no such thing as public opinion. There is only published opinion."*
Winston Churchill

CHAPTER 8

ROBERT MONTGOMERY

R obert Montgomery is a Scottish-born, London based sculptor and poet, known for his site-specific installations created from light and text. Montgomery works in a "melancholic post-Situationist" tradition, primarily in public spaces.

Born: 1972, Chapelhall Education: Edinburgh College of Art
Known for: Poetry, Installation art.

Montgomery left (Edinburgh College of Art) with a first undergraduate degree in painting and later obtained a Master of Fine Arts. While still a student he and John Ayscough applied for a grant from the Scottish Arts Council for their project, Aerial '94. They were awarded £40,000, but the grant was not intended for students, and was nearly withdrawn. Andrew Nairne (then Visual Director at the Scottish Arts Council) supported the aspiring artists, as a result the project went forward with the help of the grant.

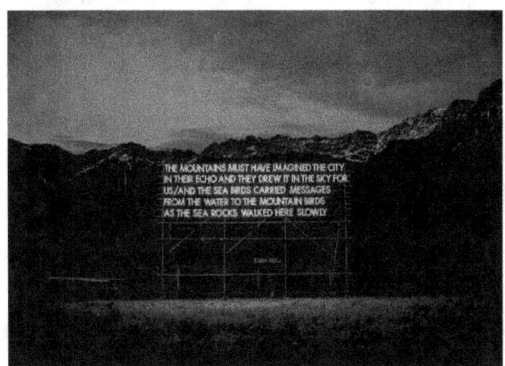

Image@robertmontgomery.org

Robert Montgomery – Poetic Billboard

Robert Montgomery creates these enormous poetic billboards set in simple type to fill urban landscapes with a little dose of poetry and magic. The ambiguous and often melancholy lines are further emphasized when lit up with crisp neon or set on fire to burn away into the night, with letters slowly dropping off into ashes as they char.

EXAMPLES of ART- BOLLOCKESE*:-

Comments from 'Art Experts' re. The Work's of ROBERT MONTGOMERY:

Article from The Guardian (UK) National Newspaper 20 March 2016 :
" He has been called a vandal, a street artist, a post-Situationist, a punk artist and the text-art Banksy. Scottish poet Robert Montgomery has consciously made an "awkward space" for himself in between artistic categories – and he thoroughly enjoys it. His work puts poetry in front of people in eye-catching visual formats: from advertising billboards he has covered with poems, to words he has set on fire or lit with recycled sunlight in public spaces – including the Sussex seafront and a Berlin airport. Recently, he has been working on today's World Poetry Day "Pay with a poem" campaign, through which customers can get coffee in exchange for poetry in cafes across the globe. Montgomery will then collect the public's poems to create an installation in a secret location....

The texts tend to be lyrical, dreamy and almost optimistic. "I feel it's a kind of responsibility to critique things that you think are bad – but I also feel an almost moral obligation to propagate hope," he says. A new global crisis has propelled him to focus his work on climate change and collaborate with the Climate Coalition. "I think the ecological crisis we are facing is the major historical crisis of our time and our generation will be judged on it."

By putting poetry in our faces, Montgomery hopes to bring it into the public discourse. "I'm interested in Roland Barthes's idea that mythology is essentially a type of speech, and that speech defines a culture. Poetry can define the dominant languages we have in culture – and now those languages are advertising and the news media."

Despite his art being displayed in the most physical of ways, he also approves of another kind of page-leaping phenomenon: the proliferation of "Instagram poets" who also, to a degree, mix the written word with careful visual presentations. "The internet is a wonderful medium for poetry," he says. "I don't think that was the idea of its creators, but it has been a really nice side-effect." He celebrates the fact

---

* **BOLLOCKESE** - Nonsensical verbiage or high-brow language used to communicate; unproven or biased opinion or an exaggerated truth; by a person who possesses or has pretensions of superior learning to project or promote items or concepts.

that self-publishing is becoming essential online, and that these peer-to-peer demographics mean poets garner audiences that "bring their work alive" before they get a chance to get published.

His work seems to have developed into the realm of inspirational quotes for fans, with his poems often popping up on their selfies, clothes, walls ... and bodies. "Getting institutional recognition is great, but someone getting tattooed is such a personal compliment. My studio is gathering some of the tattoo examples. After all, the goal of art is, for me, to communicate our innermost feelings to strangers..."

Article by Art Columnist from: The Aesthete Web-Site :

" For over a decade, Montgomery has been replacing ad pitches with poetry and presenting commentary on everything from consumerism to beauty in bold white type set against a black background. Though not really a street artist, Montgomery takes inspiration from the Situationist tradition of détournement—capturing the audience's attention in unexpected ways within the public realm. "Sometimes I will draft things in two different ways, and put it on Facebook and see which gets the most likes and then I'm like, OK, I'll do it that way," he says, sipping his beer and taking another drag off Johnny Depp.

Indeed, people no longer log on and log off the internet, they live in it—and for Montgomery, this is like having a sounding board for his work in progress 24 hours a day. "My work got out into the gallery system via the internet," he says. Facebook, he says, where fans had posted photos of his guerilla billboard work on their personal pages, is essentially where his work "entered the art system." He explains further, "It's like my peer group selected the work, as opposed to a museum director who is the age of your parents."

Montgomery also relies heavily on the art of drunk-texting to inspire his work. "You send yourself a text message at 2 in the morning coming home drunk from a party, from the back of a taxi, and the next day you decide if its madness or not," he says, glancing at his iPhone. "If it is madness you still keep it!" If only we could *all* stagger through life, smashed with epiphanies that become great artwork—would there even be room for all of our drunken work to be displayed?

"Poetry in the digital age is fascinating," says Montgomery. "I love this idea that technology is not just something we use for business emails, but actually digital media is a great new medium for poetry. That excites me quite a lot. I love that I can write a short poem and someone 2,000 miles away can see it 10 minutes later—it's amazing." In an age abounding in everything but attention spans, Montgomery's short often truism-laced phrases couldn't have arrived at a better time.

Earlier this month, Montgomery had his first solo show at C24 in Chelsea featuring his text-based installation works gathered to date; free flowing billboard displays, scrolling cryptic mottoes and aphorisms— most which can be found within the public landscape on the streets of Berlin, London and Paris. On opening night, Michael Stipe, who is an important "mythical figure" to Montgomery, came and bought his first piece.

Despite an often anti-capitalist slant, Montgomery's pieces have managed to span the divide between the 1 percent and the 99 percent— the haves and have-nots. While his billboards became the mantra of London's anti-capitalist Occupy movement back in 2012, in the same year his 2009 light piece, WHENEVER YOU SEE THE SUN REFLECTED IN THE WINDOW OF A BUILDING IT IS AN ANGEL, was selected by Dior menswear designer Kris van Assche to front the Dior Homme store in Soho, New York.

Does he feel more like a poet or an artist? Neither, really. "I didn't study literature in university, I studied art. And I didn't set out to be a poet with a capital P," Montgomery says. Critics have compared his work to the great pioneers of text-based art, Jenny Holzer and Lawrence Weiner, both of whom Montgomery credits as his inspirations, although he has long since given up heeding the words of critics…"

JOE C.THREWITT re. The Work's of ROBERT MONTGOMERY:

Tell me; what right does Mr Montgomery, or any particular group championing a self-indulgence, have to erect such a load of old nonsense in front of anything, let alone a picturesque view of a mountain range…It just beggars belief! Also in this particular instance, the bollockese merchants supporting Mr Montgomery's self promoting eye-sores should be ashamed of themselves.

This concept of so-called Art, clearly demonstrates how the boundaries have become blurred between what should be determined poetic art and visual art. Mr Montgomery may well possess qualities as a poet but by shoving his words in your face, lit up and large, doesn't make him a Shakespeare and definitely not a Rembrandt. If he was that good a poet, surely 'Arial font size 12' would suffice… it was good enough for Milton and Keats!

It's a fact; some people don't like, or even get, poetry, so who do the persons involved in erecting these word-nonsense monstrosities think they are. If we all decided to express our wordy feeling on illuminated billboards that cover nature's wonders, one should ask; what is the point of the rule of law. Also, what's surprising here is: These arty poetic individuals are usually the first to jump on the eco-friendly band-wagon. And yep Montgomery is no different, spouting his bollockese views on climate change; *"I think the ecological crisis we are facing is the major historical crisis of our time and our generation will be judged on it."* So lighting up the night sky with neon's or even worse with fire and smoke is now okay for this self-proclaimed eco-warrior…Why? Because the intellectuals have deemed it as Art. This bollockese old guff is, and should be, laughable to anyone with any true sense or ecological understanding.

The question however is how-come Mr Montgomery can get away with this?

You got it; the theme is now coming across loud-and-clear… Art bollockese from intellectuals supporting such works seem able to cut through not only common sense and decency, but long standing British laws. It is also of note with the Montgomery works and with many other self promoting, self indulgent so called artists; they themselves expel huge amounts of bollockese. Often they are just regurgitating nonsense descriptive clap-trap spoken or written by art intellectuals relative to some other works…*"I love the idea.."* , *"lyrical, dreamy and almost optimistic…"* are examples of just a few. Or maybe they too just click on the 'Instant Art Critique Phrase Generator' web-site…Go on have a look, it does actually exists.

What is another worry with regard to Mr Montgomery's intellectual commentator's, is they are attempting to brand him as a champion of social comment. They even compare him with the visual artist Banksy, because he highjacks public spaces. However, what the arty boffs have failed to pick up on; Banksy usual choice of space lacks criminal credence, in that they normally occupy dilapidated or secretive locations. Therefore although his works could be termed criminal damage, as with any graffiti not commissioned by their chosen back-drop owner, because the visual creation does not diminish the aesthetics of the wall or space they occupy, and they are often amusing, therefore no one gives a monkeys. This is definitely not the case with Mr Montgomery, because his 'guerrilla works' are placed against back-drops with far better aesthetic value than his few chosen banal words on a billboard...contrary to the mentioned bollockese:

"His work puts poetry in front of people in eye-catching visual formats: from advertising billboards he has covered with poems, to words he has set on fire or lit with recycled sunlight in public spaces – including the Sussex seafront and a Berlin airport."

And, what about the following load of gushing bollockese using the favourite cliché; *"taking inspiration..."*, topped-up with an attempt to make Mr Montgomery a cool modern dude and then ending it with a celebrity name drop....Yuk..Puke; it makes a reasonable person want to vomit!:

"Montgomery takes inspiration from the Situationist tradition of détournement—capturing the audience's attention in unexpected ways within the public realm. "Sometimes I will draft things in two different ways, and put it on Facebook and see which gets the most likes and then I'm like, OK, I'll do it that way," he says, sipping his beer and taking another drag off Johnny Depp."

Here's a question: What makes a good poet? A good visual artist seems much easier to determine than a poet. The visual image, as per the definition(s), should possess creativity, skill and visual pleasure or meaning. With poetry lets be honest, most believe 90% of it is bla..bla..bollockese anyhow. Yes a few lines may say something profound if you're tuned in to it, but on the whole, admit it, most of it make us yawn after the first paragraph.. unless it's a limerick or you're a recipient of a personal sonnet. Mr Montgomery's ditties may seem profound to him but do appear to lack innovation compared to past poets, whom lets face over the years, have written about almost every emotion and sentiment there is. It also appears Montgomery, by adopting an anti-establishment persona, has successfully recruited similar minded arty-intellectuals whom are probably searching for social protest adulation like their mums and dads did at Woodstock.

So to conclude; Mr Montgomery as a poet, may-be okay.. but as he must feel nobody wants to read his words in an accepted format on a page in a book.. even his talent as a wordsmith would seem doubtful. However as for Mr Montgomery bollockese claims as a visual artist ...would the real Monty please drive his tank right through them.

Joe's Quote of Note for Mr Montgomery and his billboard poetry:
"No work of art puts forward views. Views belong to people who are not artists." **Oscar Wilde**

CHAPTER 9

MARINA ABRAMOVIC

Marina Abramović is a Yugoslavia-born performance artist based in New York. Her work explores the relationship between performer and audience, the limits of the body, and the possibilities of the mind. Active for over three decades, Abramović has been described as the "grandmother of performance art." She pioneered a new notion of identity by bringing in the participation of observers, focusing on "confronting pain, blood, and physical limits of the body."

Marina Abramović was born in Belgrade, Yugoslavia on November 30, 1946.

From 1990–1991 Abramović was a visiting professor at the *Académie des Beaux-Arts* in Paris and at the *Berlin University of the Arts*. From 1992–1996 she was a visiting professor at the *Hochschule für bildende Künste Hamburg* and from 1997–2004 she was a professor for performance-art at the *Hochschule für bildende Künste Braunschweig. Source Wikipedia.*

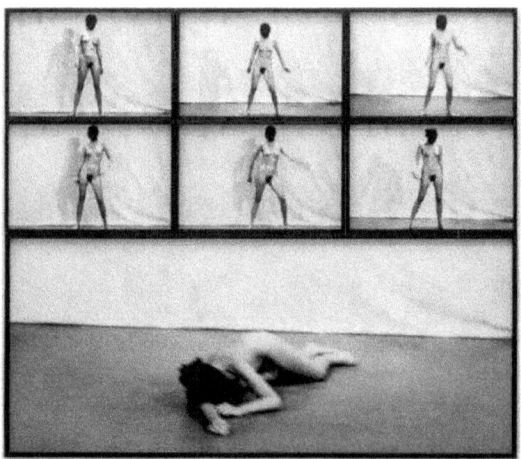

Photo@gwilymphotography.wordpress.com

Marina Abramovic – 'Freeing the Body' (1975)

Performing Art

EXAMPLES of ART- BOLLOCKESE*:-

Comments from 'Art Experts' re. The Work's of MARINA ABROMVIC:

Article from The Daily Telegraph - re: "Marina Abramovic Exhibition '512 hours' " 24 Sep 2014 :

" As per that show's title, Abramovic spent 512 hours (eight hours a day, six days a week for three months) roaming the gallery and ushering visitors around it like playthings....

She claims the "incredible" experience was worth any aches and pains, though. Some 120, 000 Londoners visited her, many of them queuing for hours and **all of them surrendering their phones, bags and other belongings** at the entrance – so as to be 100 per cent engaged. The artist claimed to offer a "positive transfer of energy", amongst other things, yet the critical reception was mixed....

....And the Lisson show is interesting for the background it provides as to how and where the Marina phenomenon began, how a young girl from Eastern Europe ended up on this year's Time 100 list and hanging out with Lady Gaga.

The key seems to be childhood oppression. In a series of performance works called "Freeing", Abramovic let herself go completely. In **Freeing the Body**, she wrapped her head in a black scarf and danced frenetically to the rhythms of a bongo drum – until she collapsed in exhaustion. In Freeing the Voice, she lay prone on a mattress and howled for three hours, till she lost her voice. And in Freeing the Memory, she uttered every word she could think of, continuously, for 50 minutes.

The first two works are recaptured in little-seen photos, while for Freeing the Memory there's an archive video – and what appears at first to be a random sequence of utterances soon reveals personally potent word-associations: from Stalin to influenza. Towards the end, the strain of recollection starts to appear on Marina's face.

---

* **BOLLOCKESE** - Nonsensical verbiage or high-brow language used to communicate; unproven or biased opinion or an exaggerated truth; by a person who possesses or has pretensions of superior learning to project or promote items or concepts.

It's startling to see a human being push themselves quite to the limit like this. The Freeing works also all had to be completed before 10pm, as that was the curfew time Mrs Abramovic had set for getting home.

Were these early performance works, then, a case of Marina throwing off the shackles imposed by both her mother and country. "Oh, yes. My mother was incredibly cold", she says, "but the Communist discipline and iron will-power she instilled made me the artist I am". Marina left home aged 29, for Amsterdam, never to return.

She insists, back then, she was "just a young artist trying things, with no idea where her art was heading". But one might easily connect 512 Hours – according to Abramovic, a rebellion against the commodification of art today – with her rebellion against authority in the Freeing works.

Perhaps Abramovic's most famous performance was Rhythm 5, in which she constructed a five–point star (that Communist symbol) out of wood on the gallery floor, soaked it in petrol and set it alight. Upon lying down in its centre, she soon passed out through lack of oxygen and was only rescued in the nick of time by a member of the audience who realised that wasn't part of the act.

This has gone down in myth as one of the great moments in performance art history, and the Lisson curators have done wonders unearthing a film of that evening. Remarkably, it's even more dramatic than I'd imagined: after ritualistically cutting her nails and hair and adding them to the pyre, Marina adopts a star-shape posture herself and, banshee-like, embraces the flame.

For those of us not entirely comfortable with the whiff of narcissism about her art today, the early performance works remind us it actually stems from something quite the opposite: self-liberation. A charitable person might even say Abramovic found her freedom and now wants to help us find ours…"

Extract from an article from the 'Artnet' Web-Site - "Marina Abramovic New York Exhibition 'The Artist is Present'" :

" Marina Abramovic's large-scale 40-year retrospective at the Museum of Modern Art, "The Artist Is Present" -- featuring Abramovic herself, seated in queenly fashion in the museum's atrium, nude performers re-creating her past work, and lots of audience participation -- has turned the usually introspective institutional sphere into an existential circus of bizarre self-help.

People have engaged with this work in ways that are as intense and profound as their interactions with paintings and sculpture. It is especially thrilling that no Mayor Giuliani equivalent showed up to close the institution because it offended us or him. That Abramovic's show is a hit proves that art is bigger than moralism, and that the audience is more open and more mature than ever. As hokey and self-centered as "The Artist Is Present" sometimes is, it also tells us that when sensationalism takes center stage, it doesn't have to be flashy, tacky, shocking and silly. Well, maybe just a little bit silly..."

**Marina Abramovic (2010) -
'Reperforming Imponderabilia'**

Maria S.H.M. and Abigail Levine

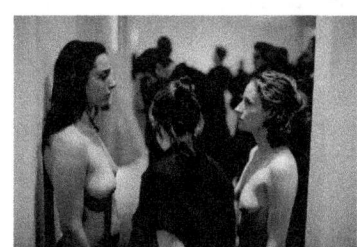

Photo: Scott Rudd.

*Extract from an article from agon.ens-lyon.fr web-site:
re. Marina Abramovic 'The Artist is Present' Exhibition at The New
York Museum of Modern Art (MoMA):*

"....The early work of many in this generation was built on the artist's specific body. Often designed for a particular place, to be fleeting—if such a thing can be said of those works that lasted anywhere from multiple hours to months—the go-for-broke ethos did not necessarily expect replication. A groundbreaking concept of late 1960s/early 1970s avant garde, asserted that the in-the-moment character of the performance, the search for experience, was paramount; that production was ephemeral, once mounted unlikely to be seen again.

6 Codification changes such performance removing an edge. Journalist Holland Cotter—"Two elements that originally defined performance art as a medium, unpredictability and ephemerality, were

missing [at MoMA]…Without them you get misrepresented history and bad theater." And, in the big-institution event in which the MoMA reperformances occurred physical risk had to be minimized. Abramović reperformer Abigail Levine explains: —"The chance and risk of Marina's early work was not there [in the MoMA show]. Risk of a certain kind had to be removed in this context, in [contracting] other bodies to do the work." Yet reperformance—repetition, duration of another kind, new rules, settings, etc—brought new understandings, new types of development, while maintaining the work's inherent surprise. These new understandings encompass a different idea of what it means for a work of performing art to continue to live. Choreographers often recreate their work. Like Monet's many visions of haystacks, versions are created for new casts, costumes changed for dancers whose technique changes the "look" of the movement. Older arts – ballet, Kabuki – know that things cannot remain static; change is the essence of performance. But performance art—with its odd blend of visual art aesthetics and the performing body is just beginning to ask what it means to preserve that which is inherently unpreservable in the way that, say, a painting is. Thus the concept of reperformance, whether the artist chooses to allow other bodies to inhabit the work or consign it to "bad video recordings" is crucial to the future of many types of performance…"

JOE C.THREWITT re. The Work's of MARINA ABRAMOVIC:

What we basically have here is people standing around naked or doing nude star jumps within a gallery space. Yep, you even get to squeeze between a couple of naked bodies as you wander around Ms Abramovic's exhibition of exhibitionists. This may be good for a giggle but is it really Art?

Ms Abramovic (hopefully no relation to the owner of Chelsea FC) claims to be a performing artist. But what is she performing? From what's on show without the addition of any written or spoken bollockese, she and her fellow exhibitionists appears to be just wandering around starkers or just posing with props, naked as a jay-bird. And as for the star jumps; they are probably a good and natural instinctive way of keeping warm in a cold gallery when minus any clothing. Therefore although Ms Abramovic is referring to what she and her co-nudies are doing as Art, let's apply a bit of common sense to this, to see if indeed it is.

We all know now what the criteria is to be determined as Art. So let us examine Ms Abramovic's works to see where her nude dancing or inert bods fit in with this.

Are the images or nude performances *creative*? Hmmm, well I suppose the fact you are either willing to stand around naked yourself, or alternatively convince others to stand around in their birthday suits, could be creative in some sort of way. Nevertheless does this creativity possess any skill? We all have skin and bits, some more pert than others, and most can walk, stand, lie down and even place a bag over their face if that's what takes their fancy. Therefore its reasonable to assess the skill element to Ms Ambrovic's works is certainly limited to say the least.

What about *elements of beauty or the portraying of matters of importance* in her works? Here we go again… that sex thing!
When it comes to the human body we all know peoples tastes differ, and thank god we do, otherwise we would all be fighting over the few Aphrodite's and Adonis's out there. So there is a good chance, one or, many of us will find some beauty in what Ms Abramovic has on display, whatever their shape, stature or endowment. Therefore does Ms Abamovic's nude bodies possess some beauty.. I suppose that's got to be a 'Yes' unless you have an adversity to certain human forms.

With regard to the question of; *portraying something of importance*? Although art intellectual spouting bollockese may rattle on about, *"freeing the body and soul"*…and *"releasing the shackles of communist disciplines"*, basically walking around in the buff and putting a bag over ones head, is such an obscure means of conveying this, without the bollockese no one would have the foggiest of what occurring. People would just think they've walked in on some care institute escapees. Therefore what begs the question here is, what came first; the idea by the exhibitionists to cavort naked or the excuse to do so? In truth it's another load of nonsense and let's face it, the likelihood is; persons who have taken time out to view Ms Abramovic's works, have probably done so for a laugh or a voyeuristic kick comforted that they won't be called perverted because the boffins have termed it 'Art'.

While writing this, I have just listened to the news in which the American President; Donald Trump on being accused of philandering with ladies of ill-repute in a Moscow hotel room, claimed he wouldn't do such a thing because he is a *'Germaphobe'*. So, there's one chap who won't be sidling passed any of the nudes in Ms Abramovic's exhibitions. This also raises the point that, not only do the art intellectuals actively assist breaches in the law, they also promote the flouting of 'health & safety' issues such intimacy in galleries may cause. Which given our passion for such regulation and rules, must be seen as truly amazing.

Okay, to sum up Ms Abramovic's performance exhibitions; yes they are nonsense which should be performed in a theatre and not wasting space in our art galleries. The time and space occupied by this exhibitionist tosh, could be set aside for the many good visual artists out there who can't find a gallery slot for love nor money. Such visual artists may have the talent, but they do not possess the support of sufficient art intellectual's spouting favourable bollockese on their behalf now increasingly necessary for success.

On the other hand.. maybe we should thank the gallery owners for allowing Ms Abramovic and her associates to cavort around with their bits out, star-jumping, wearing scarf's over their faces and frantically playing the bongos…As this is definitely a great example of providing these odd-bod exhibitionists with some well needed 'care in the community'!

Joe's Quote of Note for Ms Abramovic and her Exhibitionism: *"Shyness and modesty in men is an excellent virtue, but shyness and modesty in women is even more so."* ***Abu Bakr***

CHAPTER 10

DAMIEN HIRST

D amien Steven Hirst is an English artist, entrepreneur, and art collector. He is the most prominent member of the group known as the Young British Artists, who dominated the art scene in the UK during the 1990s.

Born: 7 June 1965, Bristol

Influenced by: Jeff Koons, Andy Warhol, Marcel Duchamp, Francis Bacon, Michael Craig-Martin, Sex Pistols, John LeKay
Education: University of London, Goldsmiths, University of London, Allerton Grange School, Leeds College of Art
Awards: Turner Prize

Death is a central theme in Hirst's works. He became famous for a series of artworks in which dead animals (including a shark, a sheep and a cow) are preserved—sometimes having been dissected—in formaldehyde. The best known of these was *The Physical Impossibility of Death in the Mind of Someone Living*, a 14-foot (4.3 m) tiger shark immersed in formaldehyde in a vitrine (clear display case). He has also made "spin paintings," created on a spinning circular surface, and "spot paintings", which are rows of randomly coloured circles created by his assistants. *Source Wikipedia.*

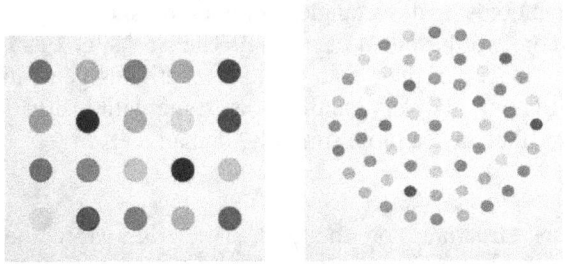

Image@MoMa.co.uk

Damien Hirst's Spot Paintings
Originally painted directly onto walls

Those versions created by Damien Hirst (himself) have been purchased for between $53,000 and $1.7 million.

EXAMPLES of ART- BOLLOCKESE*:-

Comments from 'Art Experts' re. The Work's of DAMIEN HIRST:

Extract from The Guardian (UK) Web-Site Thursday 12 January 2012:

"The titles of Damien Hirst's spot paintings give them a slightly menacing and dangerously attractive air: Cocaine Hydrochloride, Morphine Sulphate, Bovine Albumin, Butulinium Toxin A. Their relentless, insistent brightness feels almost bad for you. No wonder one group of paintings is called Controlled Substances. Yet they have no discernable secrets, and that's part of the deal. Nothing more is revealed, however long you look. They're as unsatisfying as cigarettes, calming but addictive. Avoid prolonged exposure.....

....Hirst's spots soon acquired a clean and emphatic air. These were take-it-or-leave-it paintings, without problems or doubts, painted directly on the wall. He was doing lots of other things at the time, including painting on discarded cardboard boxes and producing his first medicine cabinets. The variety and inventiveness was evidence of an enquiring and lively mind. Lots of artists could make a whole career from such an apparently limited repertoire of forms and effects. But Hirst, of course, keeps several artistic modes running at once. This spring, a retrospective opens at Tate Modern, while Hirst intends to open his own museum in London's Vauxhall some time soon.

No matter how many spot paintings there are – tondos, triangles, squares, rhomboids and rectangles with corners cut off – there will always be more words spilled over them. The works look as if they were generated by machine, their cold random repetitions generating endless sameness. It is only the very small works, some with just half a dot on a tiddly canvas, that have a more sprightly, human feel.

All are structured on the grid. The grid, wrote the US critic Rosalind Krauss, is what art looks like when it turns its back on nature. The pleasures of Hirst's pharmaceutical paintings, as the spots are generically titled, are as artificial as chemicals and drugs. Showing them

---

* **BOLLOCKESE** - Nonsensical verbiage or high-brow language used to communicate; unproven or biased opinion or an exaggerated truth; by a person who possesses or has pretensions of superior learning to project or promote items or concepts.

all over the world at the same time becomes part of their content and meaning: they're infiltrating everywhere, their field expanding to cover the world.

For a while, coloured spots signalled a fresh, sophisticated, zesty new Britain. Whether Hirst had much to do with this is uncertain. No one owns the spot, although designer appropriations always remind you of Hirst, or of the Japanese artist Yayoi Kusama, who has been covering her work, and her body, in polka dots for 60 years. (Kusama is at Tate Modern next month.) US artist Ellsworth Kelly was also arranging grids of colours in the 1950s, while Germany's Gerhard Richter has been painting colour charts and squares for decades. Hirst just ran with an unoriginal idea in an original way. Which, pretty much, is what art always does..."

Extract from The Guardian (UK) Web-Site Friday 16 March 2012:

" As Hirst has become wealthier, his work, which (as Houellebecq points out) incessantly circles the twin poles of death and money, has lost the cocoon of edgy cool that sheltered it through the 90s, to emerge, like one of his murdered butterflies, in its full form: as a pure commodity, fluttering free of the things that tie most art down – aesthetics, geography, the specifics of material and manufacture. He has certain signature elements (dots, pills, dead things, shiny shelves, chunks of scientific text) that can be deployed, with minor variations, at every price point from major installation to souvenir mug. His thematic interests in pop culture, shock and replication make it easy to keep a straight face while he sells his dodgier diffusion lines in markets that haven't been saturated by the earlier "better" work – see, for example, the shameless recent series of National Geographic-style butterfly photos, punted out in Hong Kong, safely away from the derision that might have accompanied them in London or New York.

This isn't just art that exists in the market, or is "about" the market. This is art that *is* the market – a series of gestures that are made wholly or primarily to capture and embody financial value, and only secondarily have any other function or virtue. Hirst has gone way beyond Warhol's explorations of repetition and banality. Sooner or later, his advisers will surely find a way for him to dispense with the actual objects altogether and he will package concepts in tranches, like mortgage securities, some good stuff with some trash, to be traded on the *bourse* in Miami-Basel.

For the moment, Hirst still has to make things and we still have to look at them. The byproduct of his activities is the most starkly authoritarian corpus of art of recent times. All those hard, glittering surfaces, those rotting animals. The body, for Hirst, is trash, which exists to be anatomised, displayed, described in cribbed Latin names. The only way to cheat death is to slough off your rotting flesh and take on the qualities of capital. It's the 21st-century version of *ars longa*, *vita brevis*. Don't just make money, *be money*: weightless, ubiquitous, infinitely circulating, immortal…"

Extract taken from the 'Quora' web-site:

"…Many on the internet are simply looking to have their *pet peeves* supported. Yeah, I know, he's a billionaire and most artists don't make a dime from their artwork. But -if you really want an interpretation of the Spot paintings -read on...

Throughout history painters have applied colors next to each other to great effect. The colors Van Gogh combined give his work tremendous power. As in nature, even one color next to another can be entrancing. (Orange sunset clouds against a blue sky.) As some western/European painting became more and more abstracted, it got to the point where there were no objects represented. Yet the artist may still be representing certain ideas or emotions. After the abstract expressionist's period, people began questioning interpretation. As in: does that red brush stroke really mean the same to me as it meant to the artist? Each viewer coming from a whole different set of life experiences- maybe even a different culture. Each mark will have a different meaning or feeling to each viewer.

Damien Hurst has eliminated the shape as an issue. The uniformity of the spots takes care of that. Acknowledging that the viewer completes the experience, he is randomly placing colors next to each other. Random individuals will experience the juxtapositions of color in their own way…"

Extract taken from facebook.com – "How the chance meeting of Dave Stewart and Damien Hirst led to a new song and a spot-painting":

" Damien Hirst met Dave Stewart in the early 1990s at the opening of a group exhibition in London's Docklands, where Hirst and Angus Fairhurst staged Freeze in 1988....

Hirst created his first versions of the spot paintings painted directly onto the walls of the warehouse in his exhibition Freeze in 1988. The first works on canvas date from the early 1990s and they were made in parallel with the Medicine Cabinets and the Pill Cabinets. Belonging to this earliest group of works on canvas, Being God (for Dave) and Acridine both betray the hand made quality of Hirst's earliest paintings, despite their purported automation. Throughout his career, Hirst has been preoccupied with colour which, on a formal level, he interrogates in the pharmaceutical paintings. Self-restricted by a grid, the only variation is the colour and tone of the dots, which, according to the formula, remain perennially unrelated while enticing the eye to find patterns, a futile exercise which is symptomatic of our desperate desire to establish order from the chaos of nature. The smaller the dots and the greater their replication, the more they vie against the retina and play with our spatialawareness. This is particularly evident in Being God (for Dave) where the 930 spots create a dizzying chromatic grid. Incredibly rare in this scale, there are only three larger paintings with one-inch spots in Hirst's 1997 catalogue.

Like the sculptural works, the kaleidoscopic paintings express Damien's life-long fascination with the medical sciences and the enormity of the accomplishment of modern science in its attempt to prolong the inevitability of death. In the pharmaceutical paintings, the panoply of coloured dots stands in for the myriad pills and palliatives that mankind has developed to blunt the ravages of disease and prolong life. As such, the pharmaceutical paintings enshrine the fundamental tenets of Hirst's entire oeuvre, by interrogating the common ground between the traditionally distinct and antithetical faculties of science and art. In a pseudo-deification of medicine, Hirst taps into our blind credence in the restorative powers of these chemically engineered life-givers.

In the process, he highlights the usurpation of spiritual faith by modern faith in drugs. In the vacuum left behind by the decline of organised religion in the modern world, Hirst presents us with a new pantheon of saints for our adulation, each individually named and endowed with its own unique healing power. While the other paintings in the series, such as Acridine, are named after specific substances, the title of this painting, Being God, references mankind's ambition to cheat death and outdo nature, to use chemistry and the life sciences to break the ordained cycle of life and death…"

Extract taken from archiv.ub.uni-heidelberg.de web site – "Reflections of consumerism in Damien Hirst's Spot Paintings" :

"….Hirst's spots … are abstract and concrete at the same time, another contradiction. The word 'spot' can per se name something dirty, something unwanted, unplanned, human, individual that accidently happens which is a contradiction to the clean and mechanical visual appearance of the spots, which are executed by assistants, who are - though individuals–between a tool, a machine and the artist Hirst, who still chooses the colors for each spot painting, who creates paintings, individual artworks and produces consumer goods for "over the sofa" at the same time. "Over the sofa" is a name of one of the artist - entrepreneur Hirst's companies, the name ironically quotes the era of the artwork as a commodity. Spot paintings, i.e. paintings in general, these old-fashioned and timeless art objects are perfect forthis "age of art as a commodity".

Since the mid-1990s Hirst speaks of ending painting series like the spots, but never does. Maybe he was inspired by Warhol, who did the same (or did not). This behavior mirrors the much-vaunted "death of painting", which he neither confirms nor denies. For Hirst painting is probably the artistic medium par excellence, as it is for Jeff Koons: "A photograph for me does not have the same spiritual seduction, it does not have the same essence.

" Asked what makes painting more "eternal" than photos".. Koons answers: "For one thing you have the support of the museum. And the framework of painting, and the support of the institution of museums, is in everyone, it's in the subconscious mind ". They function as "fetishes, paintings about fetishes and about painting as fetish and they offend and flatter simultaneously. There is a […] [spot painting] for every collector's taste if not perhaps pocketbook."

Conversely the spots look like art under a microscope, individual pigments on asurface. The status of painting itself as an object is discussed, through the use of pure geometric primitives - color and form-the "myths of originality and authencity", which are so important for the art market, are almost revealed almost scientifically, in other words, "abstraction's mystery" is eliminated by the "endgame painter" Hirst. The same can be said for his series Butterfly or Spin Paintings. By paying a tribute to, stealing or quoting formally from the 1960s and 1970s Hirst places himself in art history. Although Hirst's spots appear like dots of Armleder, Gernes or Downing, a detail of a Lichtenstein or a quote of Richter, they are different. Richter did paintings in which he replicated, in large scale, industrial color charts produced by paint manufacturers. As with his photo-paintings, the use of found material as a source removed the subjective compositional preferences of the artist. The Color Chart Paintings took this a step further, eradicating any hierarchy of subject or representational intent, and focusing on color to create an egalitarian language of art. Unlike Richter Hirst chooses the colors himself, but lets assistants paint, Richter painted himself. Richter called his Color Chart Paintings "1024 Colours" or similar, Paul Gernes and Armleder called theirs "Untitled", Downing his "Grit #8", to support similar ideas of serious, idealistic but for us today a little mechanical democracy - what you see is what you get. With erasing content and individual artistic style these dot paintings like Hirst's…"

 JOE C.THREWITT re. The Work's of DAMIEN HIRST:

Its common knowledge Mr Damien Hirst has created many works other than the 'spot paintings' being remarked on here, including his pickled dead animals, fly infested installations and diamond incrusted skulls. All these works are accompanied by masses of art-bollockese by so-called intellectuals, which no doubt will come under my scrutiny in later books. However, for this edition let's just focus on the zit-pics of which there has been in excess of 1000 versions produced under the direction of Hirst, but only 5 by the man himself!

It is of note when looking at Mr Hirst's history, initially the bollockese was all positive, with him being bigged-up by all-un-sundry in the art world. He of course was one of the *Young British Artists* helped by the Saatchi marketing machine to gain notoriety along with *Tracey Emin* and the rest of the gang in the project. Nevertheless, when Hirst's works started to sell on an industrial scale, due to mass-production, he started making a fortune. Whether it's true or not, his patrons didn't apparently like this accumulation of wealth as it wasn't in their control. The joke being, they may have created the monster (*this disputed by Hirst*), but allegedly not being able to restrain the beast and his resulting increase in wealth, things all went pear-shape with Damo falling out big-time with the marketing guru resulting in him not wanting his works exhibited in the guru's gallery.

Anyhow, Mr Hirst rode the storm and successfully carried on with his industrial sales push of his works and image. Today it is said he is the highest living earner in the Art business. And, although they say money can't buy happiness, it sure helps get you some praise and positive bollockese to counter the bad....That's this commentators take on the Damo's story in brief...now let's look at the colourful zit-pics that helped the boy become a very rich man.

When first viewing Mr Hirst's spot paintings you may think they are just a random collection of coloured-in circles. I certainly did and therefore reasonably assumed these were just another child-like set of pictures by another *Young British Artist* subject of a marketing experiment. But the spots aren't random at all. They actually portray scientific elements, mineral and chemical, with the colour of the spots corresponding to the mineral or chemical they represent relative to the periodic table...yep pretty innovative you could say!

This interpretation certainly transformed the works from meaningless to meaningful, and unlike most bollockese, these claims can be factually evidenced by anyone with a CSE in chemistry. The works are also pleasing to the eye, even when their purported purpose is lost. And, although they appear simplistic, there is some skill in creating a perfect circle of colour without ragged edges.. you try it; you will definitely require some precision cut, low-tac stencils. So basically, without any intellectual art-bollockese what-so-ever, Mr Hirst's spotty pictures can be viewed with their colourful visual content for simple enjoyment. This enjoyment enhanced when the viewer is made aware of the scientific link, however tenuous.

Reading some of the zit-pic bollockese examples they certainly show these so-called art-intellectual have missed the obvious spot *(excuse the pun...again)*. Have a read of this load of bla..bla..yuk:

"....Hirst's spots ... are abstract and concrete at the same time, another contradiction. The word 'spot' can per se name something dirty, somethingunwanted, unplanned, human, individual that accidentally happens which is a contradiction to the clean and mechanical visual appearance of the spots..."
Jeeez.. what absolute tosh!

What has to be admired is there is a zit-picture, colour matched to fit every zit-faced student's bedroom wall, reproduced at a price their parents are happy to fork out. Colourful and simple pictures that have been marketed with their scientific link as intellectually cool. Yep the boy cracked it..chetttingggg...$$$$.

Therefore, you could reasonably ask the question; why does Damo need all that art-bollockese when his popularist zit-pics seemingly sell themselves? The answer probably is because his rise to notoriety was engineered by marketing bollockese and lets face it most of his other works are arguably so off-the-wall there're reliant on it.

You will have noticed in Mr Hirst's biography, he is recorded as an 'Artist' and an 'Entrepreneur'. This should really record him as an 'entrepreneur in the art business'.. end of. The guy, having been given the leg-up to kick start his career has taken it by the balls and milked every bit of his talent for great financial gain. But his talent really lies in his ability to sell and market his conceptual ideas, not the actual creation of his so-called art works. Most of which are knocked up by his team of paid flunkies… Actually it's wrong to call these people flunkies, as they are probably accomplished artists in their own right whom have not been afforded the opportunities of their pay-master. Nevertheless, this takes nothing away from the fact that Mr Hirst having conceived the science linked zit-pics, then saw the populist appeal and exploited it.

Let's be quite clear here, Damien Hirst is an excellent entrepreneur. He has made the very best of the opportunity he was fortunate to be afforded. As his wealth has escalated, it is of note his crazy concepts have reflected this. The production costs of pickling creatures in large tanks, can't be cheap. And covering a skull in diamonds is just pure extravagant nonsense…it just makes you think the boy's a poser, no better than the city trader with a Ferrari screaming.. "Look at me I've made it".. and it doesn't matter how.

Joe's Quote of Note for Mr Hirst and his lucrative endeavours: *"Try not to become a man of success but rather a man of value."* **Mahatma Ghandi**

CHAPTER 11

ROBERT RYMAN

Robert Ryman (born May 30,1930) is an American painter identified with the movements of monochrome painting, minimalism, and conceptual art. He is best known for abstract, white-on-white paintings. He lives and works in New York.

Ryman has stated that his paintings' titles are meaningless, and that they only exist as a form of identification. Ryman actually prefers the term of "name" for a painting instead of a title because he is not creating a picture or making reference to anything except the paint and the materials. The "names" of paintings often come from the names of art supplies, companies, or are just general words that do not carry much connotation. *Source Wikipedia.*

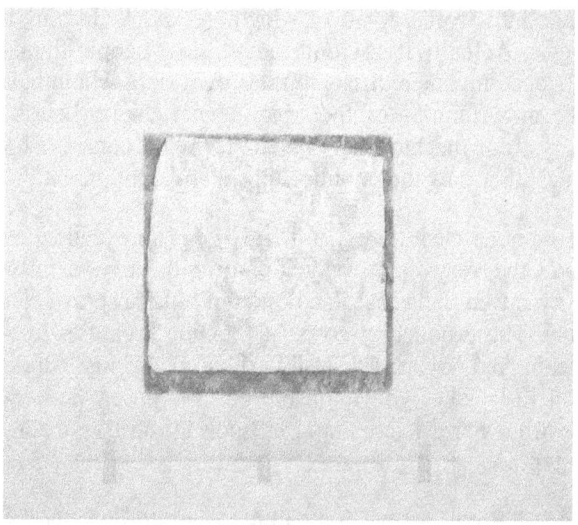

Image@deidreadams.com

Robert Ryman – 'Surface Veil' (1970-1971)
Oil on fibreglass, 22 x 29 inches,
with waxed paper frame and masking tape.

"The real purpose of painting is to give pleasure."
–Robert Ryman

EXAMPLES of ART- BOLLOCKESE*:-

Comments from 'Art Experts' re. The Work's of ROBERT RYMAN:

Extract from www.deidreadams.com (art blog) – "Robert Ryman –
White paint, not white paintings" January 19th, 2012 :

"..The interesting thing about Ryman is how he became so well known in spite of (or because of?) his unapologetically unconventional approach to painting. He confounded the critics, who tried variously to categorize his work as minimalist, or anti-form, or process, or conceptualist, while admitting that none of these could be perfectly applied. He resists the idea that his work is abstract, saying "I don't abstract from anything. [My work is] involved with real visual aspects of what you really are looking at, whether it's wood, or you see the paint, and the metal, and how it's put together and how it works with the wall and how it works with the light."

He also resisted attempts to place him into a specific box or frame within the greater art world. "I'm not involved with any kind of art movement. I'm not a scholar, I'm not a historian. I just look at it as solving problems and working on the painting and the visual experience. There is no attempt at illusion; the paintings are not "about" anything other than what's right before your eyes. What you see is what you get – nothing more, nothing less.

I read parts of *Used Paint* a couple of years ago when I was doing research for a school project. It was a treat for me soon thereafter to be able to go to the San Francisco Museum of Modern Art and see some of these paintings in person. They are just what you'd expect, but somehow in person they have a surprising presence. I'm drawn to Ryman's work aesthetically, and I admire his ability to put forth these seemingly simple objects as paintings and get them hung in the most prestigious of museums. I have an impressive number of partially finished textile works lying around my own studio, suspended from completion because I love the raw edges and I don't want to cut, bind, or hide them in some "professional" way. If I were Ryman, that would be the end of it – I'd just hand them over to the Guggenheim and up they'd go as is….

---

* **BOLLOCKESE** - Nonsensical verbiage or high-brow language used to communicate; unproven or biased opinion or an exaggerated truth; by a person who possesses or has pretensions of superior learning to project or promote items or concepts.

Ryman demonstrates how his paintings consist not only of the support and the paint, but also the edges, the fasteners, and the wall itself. He tapes panels to the walls with blue painter's tape, and then paints right over the tape and onto the walls beneath the panels. Then the tape, which has functioned as a resist, is removed. The process is repeated multiple times. This creates a variance in the surface and edge surrounding each panel. The quality of the light in the room is extremely important to the aesthetic experience, including how it changes throughout the day…"

An installation of Robert Ryman works at the Saatchi Gallery, London. *(Courtesy Saatchi Gallery)*

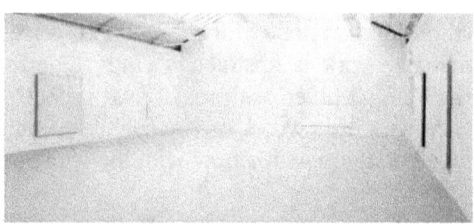

Taken from The Independent (UK) Newspaper - "Robert Ryman paints in any colour, so long as it's white" Tuesday 16 February 1993:

"..For Nicholas Serota, director of the Tate Gallery, Ryman is 'one of the most important abstract painters of his generation. By limiting himself to an area of the palette, as it were, but working on all kinds of materials and surfaces, he has stretched the boundaries of painting. In particular, he has drawn attention to the importance of light in painting.'

For Massimo Carboni, writing in Contemporary Artists, 'the great majority of Robert Ryman's pictures are rectangular in shape and painted in white. They refer to nothing beyond themselves: they are simply surfaces covered with paint. Thus what comes clearly to the fore is the language, or rather the various languages, of the material, released from any obligation to depict actual existing phenomena.' For Matthew Collings, in City Limits, the problem with Ryman's all-white paintings is that 'the people who tend to go on about them divide too much into saints or philistines. The paintings themselves are a bit like that - at once inward and meditative, and all too obvious.' And for John McEwen, reviewing the 1970s Whitechapel show in the Spectator, 'Ryman's art is about sensation, the physical sensation of painting and visual sensations thus revealed . . . Ryman is at his best when he is least constructional and most painterly.'

Almost every painting in the retrospective is white, or a shade of it. Some are so minimalist that there is barely a sign of their having been touched by human hand; others are heavy with tempestuous swirling patterns in thick impasto. Some have underlayers of one or several colours - blues and greens in one, deep reds in another - subtly peeking through curving, often biomorphic forms in heavy white paint. In a number of works, the bare canvas shows through - either at the edges, almost as a frame, or peeking through the painted areas, playing with finished and unfinished surfaces. Many of these works are seductively sensuous, calming on the eye and, indeed, beautiful.

But his most minimal canvases are not 'easy' works for the uninitiated. For the benefit of those who draw a blank at what are - on the surface - blank canvases, a direct if philistine question seemed the best approach: how would he explain to the man on the street the difference between a canvas painted with white household enamel and the wall decorated in household paint by gallery staff? 'What I'm doing is different,' he said. 'I'm not doing what a wall-painter does. They wouldn't paint a wall like this. It wouldn't have this depth or size.' He giggled. 'It may look easy, but any good painting looks easy, as if no struggle was involved . . . If you look at a Matisse, it looks like he just picked up a brush and did a few strokes, as if by magic. That's the mark of a good painting.'..."

 JOE C.THREWITT re. The Work's of ROBERT RYMAN:

This chap Ryman has definitely cracked it! One of these white-on-white pictures sold in New York for $15 Million...yep $15 Million for a white canvas painted with.. yes you better believe it.. white paint. Does it pictorially portray anything? That's a blatantly obvious... No! So, surely there must be gold dust mixed with the paint? Again that's a... No! It's just a white canvas painted white. How can anyone criticize Mr Ryman, the man must be a genius. He certainly is at making money, but it does raise the question; are we the viewing public really that damn stupid not to look at these works for what they really are? White painted canvasses that contrary to Mr Ryman's claims, any painter & decorator or DIY enthusiast could knock up in 20 minutes!

So how come Mr Ryman has the genius to sell his white canvasses for such an exorbitant price, and more astonishing, why would any sane person pay such an amount?

It's all pretty simplistic really and not just the paintings. The success of Mr Ryman's white-on-white collection must be attributed to amazing marketing by the creator, art-intellectuals and art organisations. To market these works as they have, has to be the equivalent of selling fridges to Eskimos. But unlike fridges that actually perform a function, all these non-works do is steal exposure that truly creative working artists would give their hind-teeth for. Therefore, all you art-intellectual and gallery exhibitors should search your sorry souls for promoting these non-works to the detriment of other truly creative talents.

Nevertheless, the bottom line here, as with all the works mentioned in this book is; it's us 'Joe Public' that are allowing Art to be high-jacked by the conceptual crazies. We are being sold ideas, concepts and in this case; white space, by persons and organization spouting art-bollockese that should be trying to raise artistic standards, not blow them completely out of the water. The truth is; by acquiescing and thus accepting modern artworks will now always be bizarre, this over-time has allowed art-institutions to be run by art-barking conceptualists. This leaves those seeking 'visual creativity combined with skill' to be categorized detrimentally as 'traditionalists' and left to look backwards, with the only option of attending art-museums to find excellence. Basically individuals with visual common sense are now so ostracized by the art-elite and their craziness, we are frequently referred to as *philistines*...surely visually sensible people cant all be philistines? It has now got to the point we (*us philistines*) know modern galleries are going to be full of child-like art with descriptive bullshit so why give a toss. Result; modern art has become the domain of the conceptual crazy, simplistic 'ismists' and their gullible followers. This art-intellectual discrimination may be sad, but it's now apparent it is rampantly becoming the norm.

I'm sure Mr Ryman is a very nice guy, although comparing himself with Matisse must be a tongue in cheek piss-take. However, he certainly is a clever one and if he was a sales executive, as he should be acclaimed rather than an artist, he would be up-there with Richard Branson and Donald Trump (pre-president of course). Nevertheless, even as a top sales exec, he will never be as good as Bill Gates or Mr Dyson, because unlike them, his creative skill relative to his product is just like the bollockese intellectual say,.. "Minimal".

However, trying to be fair and objective, as an interior design fixture, some of Mr Rymans works would be excellent. It is envisaged many a budding banker would happily hang a white picture on a white wall in their minimalist bankside desirable residences. Ahh..but then I suppose you could argue; is a banker's idea of excellence, something you would be wise to steer well clear of?

Okay, having now looked and brought some well needed sense to Mr Ryman's actual works; let's look at some of the absolutely bizarre art-bollockese the intellectuals expect us to believe. It must be said commentators emanating from the most renown galleries, have got some of the craziest of the crazies commenting on their behalf:

"...Ryman is 'one of the most important abstract painters of his generation. By limiting himself to an area of the palette, as it were, but working on all kinds of materials and surfaces, he has stretched the boundaries of painting. In particular, he has drawn attention to the importance of light in painting.'"

This bollockese is supposedly from a top art gallery Director. This guy's CV surely must need reviewing, together with an eye-test recommendation!   Furthermore what about this ridiculous load of bollockese:

"...Robert Ryman's pictures are rectangular in shape and painted in white. They refer to nothing beyond themselves: they are simply surfaces covered with paint. Thus what comes clearly to the fore is the language, or rather the various languages, of the material, released from any obligation to depict actual existing phenomena."

Hands up if you have a scooby-doo what this guy's on about??

You may think this is completely laughable, but let's not forget; somehow Mr Ryman has sadly managed to get all these influential art-boffs on-board to promote his non-works. And although he may claim there is more to them than meets the eye, which at the best is dubious, who's having the last $15 million laugh, and while the current bollockese is being believed, investment buyers of Mr Ryman's nonsense are also having a bit of a chuckle too.

Joe's Quote of Note for Mr Ryman and his pictures of nothing: "Art is anything you can get away with." ***Marshall McLuhan***

CHAPTER 12

CY TWOMBLY

Edwin Parker "Cy" Twombly, Jr. was an American painter, sculptor and photographer. He belonged to the generation of Robert Rauschenberg and Jasper Johns but chose to live in Italy after 1957.

His paintings are predominantly large-scale, freely-scribbled, calligraphic and graffiti-like works on solid fields of mostly gray, tan, or off-white colors. Many of his works are in the permanent collections of most of the museums of modern art around the world, including the Menil Collection in Houston, the Tate Modern in London or the New York's Museum of Modern Art. He was also commissioned for the ceiling of a room of the Musée du Louvre in Paris.
Source_Wikipedia.

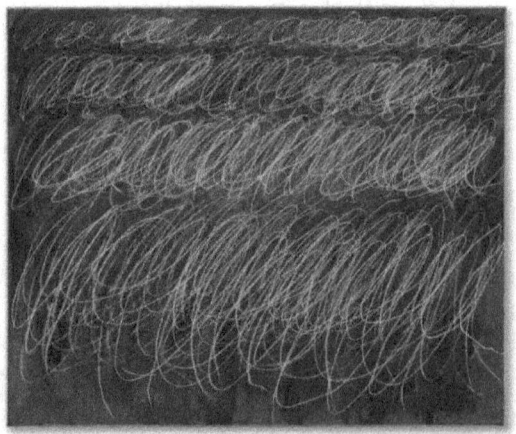

Image @ Christie's.com

Cy Twombly- Untitled (Blackboard Scribble) 1970

Created in 1970, the painting, *Untitled*, made of white wax crayon lines against a grey background, executed in four rows of exuberant scrawl

Purchase Value: $35- and $55 Million.

EXAMPLES of ART- BOLLOCKESE*:-

Comments from 'Art Experts' re. The Work's of CY TWOMBLY:

"...In 1966, Twombly began the blackboard series, named for their resemblance to a classroom chalkboard with white markings. *Untitled* came toward the end of the series when Twombly would fill entire canvases with a profusion of graphic coils using a strict process that was derived from handwriting techniques that children first learn in school..."

Extract from Cytwombly.info Web-site:

".....Twombly's return to New York in 1953, when he devised a number of strategies to thwart his skill as a draftsman and access the 'simple directness' he perceived in 'primitive' art. Whilst this quest for unmediated expression has been likened to Dubuffet and Art Brut, in Twombly it seems to be tempered with an awareness of the repetitive and referential nature of the mark. One drawing is a direct quotation from his 'North African' sketchbook, miming its look of scribbled immediacy through careful reiteration. The same 'primal' forms are reproduced in a painting of 1953 entitled Tiznit - not in reference to the North African village, but because Twombly liked the sound of the word.

This emphasis on the materiality of the signifier, as a mark or a noise produced by the body, remains evident throughout his practice. Drafted into the army in 1954, Twombly began to draw in the dark, producing lines that scratch and stutter across the page like the uncoordinated daubs of a primary-school child. Reminiscent of surrealist 'automatic' drawings, they are concerned less with yielding 'unconscious' imagery than with disengaging the skill of the draftsman through a series of bodily impediments. Alternatively drawing at oblique angles, or as though with his left hand, Twombly explored the mark as the material product of the body, or more specifically the body under duress - its habitual modes of functioning disrupted.

---

* **BOLLOCKESE** - Nonsensical verbiage or high-brow language used to communicate; unproven or biased opinion or an exaggerated truth; by a person who possesses or has pretensions of superior learning to project or promote items or concepts.

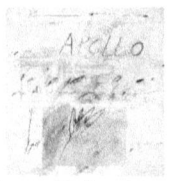

Cy Twombly
Bolsena Drawings:

'Apollo and the Artist' 1975

Image@altervista.org

There is a gap of ten years between the first room and the 1969 Bolsena drawings that follow. During that time Twombly had settled in Rome, where he moved in 1957, and the open scribbles of his early drawings had tightened into a vocabulary of scatological and pornographic graffiti.

By 1969, these scabrous marks were being filtered through his concurrent preoccupation with the Apollo space landing - so that the scattered components of the Bolsena pieces suggest vectors and compartments more than breasts, buttocks and vulvae. The omission of two 1961 drawings exhibited in St. Petersburg (and reproduced in the catalogue) thus has the effect of 'cleaning up' the Serpentine show, and making Twombly's development from 1959-69 difficult to comprehend.

This problem is compounded by a distinct lack of information, both in the exhibition itself and the glossy colour catalogue. The latter contains a gushing appreciation by historian Simon Schama, but no catalogue entries for individual works, most of which were previously unpublished. This becomes particularly problematic when regarding some smaller studies, which hint at a preparatory status without making their function explicit.

Twombly's friends Robert Rauschenberg and Jasper Johns are often credited with reintroducing Modernism's repressed terms - language, temporality, the image and the body - to American art of the fifties and sixties. In recent years there has been a sustained attempt to relocate Twombly within this American counter-tradition, with a retrospective of the paintings at the Museum of Modern Art, New York (1995), and the sculpture at the National Gallery of Art, Washington (2001). The introduction to the Serpentine exhibition - supported by the US Embassy - declares Twombly 'one of the greatest living American artists.' Yet in the 1960s his work fell out of favour with American critics, seeming to embody the decadent grandiloquence of European culture to eyes attuned to Minimalist pragmatism..."

Extract from New York Times Website - "An Artist of Selective Abandon" July 6, 2011:

"….Mr. Twombly worked with a combination of abandon and selectivity that split the difference between his two friends (*Robert Rauschenberg and Jasper Johns*). His work was in many ways infinitely more basic, even primitive, in its emphasis on direct old-fashioned mark making, except that his feverish scribbles and calligraphic scrawls made that process seem new and electric. And part of that electricity came from his ecstatic response to history, literature and other art, and the raw emotionalism that his mark making conveyed.

His rough, improvised surfaces almost invariably conveyed a startling openness and vulnerability. Whether graffitilike sex organs and orifices or blackboard-style diagrams, his scribblings felt inordinately exposed, and even unhinged, and almost suspended in midair. Interviewed by the art historian and curator Kirk Varnedoe, who organized a retrospective of Mr. Twombly's work at the Museum of Modern Art in 1994-95, the artist referred to an "irresponsibility of gravity" as central to his art.

But as abrupt and even violent as his individual works could feel, Mr. Twombly was in many ways an artist of continuity. His raw mark making could be seen as Surrealist automatism pushed to unprecedented extremes. His titles — "Vengeance of Achilles," "Leda and the Swan," "Night Watch," "School of Athens," "Thermopylae," "Lepanto" — asserted again and again that no part of culture was so old that it could not inspire new art. Living most of his adult life in Italy and building so explicitly on the achievements of "old Europe" in his work, he thoroughly blurred the divide between American and European art that many critics and art historians liked to cultivate.

Mr. Twombly even maintained continuities where Abstract Expressionism was concerned. Arguably the crux of his achievement was not so much to overturn the style as to subvert it from within. Although the Abstract Expressionists liked to believe, in the words of Barnett Newman, that "we are making it out of ourselves," Mr. Twombly in some ways beat them at their own game…."

JOE C.THREWITT re. The Work's of CY TWOMBLY:

If you didn't know better, Cy Twombly would surely seem to be a made up name. Mr Twombly after moving to Italy from New York, has undoubtedly left a legacy of hope for every doting parent, grand-parent or zoo keeper. If these scribble pics were done by Cy as an adult, then he really must have been suffering from some form of human regression syndrome...Let me explain:

Today I have had a one-way conversation with Ms Mya Smith. To my knowledge she has never met Cy or his so called mates. However, remarkably she can not only re-produce very similar works to that of Mr Towmbly, but in addition, she enhances her creations with random colours. This we understand Mr Twombly struggled with. Also, sometime to greater effect, Mya will swap the coloured crayons, being the main medium of her works, from her right hand to her left with the ability to produce equally refined results. Furthermore she often rubs biscuit type material into her works for added texture... marvellous.. and you would think given Mr Twombly's portfolio, Mya works should easily be worth $15 Million of anyone's money. Mya is my 18 month year old grand-daughter so maybe I'm a bit bias, but I'm sure any toddler you know could do just as well... if you get the gist!

This legacy of artistic hope left by Mr Twombly can also be afforded to most tree living primates. However, if they were to sell their scribbles for anything close to that allegedly obtained by Cy, there would be many a happy zoo-keeper.

Okay we can mock! Mocking is easy when the subject matter is less than what is expected by those purporting to be acclaimed for their skill. We mock footballers who miss open goals. We mock professional golfers when they do air shots and, we even mock performing artists who forget their lines. But lets be honest; it should be expected by those in superfluous careers taking big-bucks for their efforts displayed in the public domain. Especially when hard working Joe's witness dire efforts or absolute crap from such exhorted individuals who are meant to be at the top of their game.

Therefore, the question being asked here is; How the hell did Mr Twombly convince anyone claiming to be an art expert his works should be recognized as great art and therefore worth big money?

It is accepted there could be many answers, but none of them seem honourable if you view Cy Twombly's works for what they are; scribbles. It could be Mr Towmbly had influential buddies associated with renowned galleries or it could simply be he was another marketing experiment. Another thought is that he may have been the subject of a bet between competing art-intellectual or gallery boffins. Whatever the answer, it just goes to prove Art is now languishing in a institution where artistic skill has been replaced by influential bollockese.

An explanation of this betting conspiracy needs an analogy: Do you remember the television drama about a London lawyer called; Rumpole of the (Old) Baily? Well Rumpole QC used to have a running intellectual, or smart arse, game with a Judge hearing his cases. The game required them both to try and include as many classical quotations from famous authors or poets in their respective case summing-up speeches as possible, without drawing any untold attention. The person who included the most recognised quotations in their speeches won the bet. The fact the quotations would hold little or no relevance to the case being heard, but lost in the verbal legalese expected of their roles, just added to the jolly jape. This of course proved very amusing.... unless it was you in the dock! Nevertheless, it is common knowledge intellectual colleagues do play such games with each other.

Therefore, it seems reasonable to believe, given the absolute direness of Mr Twombly's scribbled works, he may well be subject of a riotous bet between some art-intellectuals guffawing at Joe Public's gullibility to accept anything they decide should be acclaimed as great art... *Although this unlikely I would love to think it was true,* as it does seem to make some sense and logical reasoning why Mr Twombly's childish creations are held in such high esteem.

These works of Cy Twombly's, like many others in this book, may leave you baffled to how they have become to be praised, let alone afforded great acclaim. The 'scribbles' by Mr Twombly do seem to epitomise all that is wrong with modern art, as without any associated bollockese these works would receive what they really should; Ridicule. These Twombly efforts and other like them, have inevitably caused budding artists with true artistic technical skill and flair, which there are many, to ask themselves; "what has this chap done to deserve such credence and notoriety when the works lack anything that could reasonably be seen as innovative or possessing an iota of skill in execution."?

This may seem harsh to those that champion Mr Twombly's works and his bollockese squad. Nevertheless it does seem reasonable to claim; anyone who believes these scribbles exhibits artistic talent to the extent advocated, clearly possess no measure of artistic truth in their soul. So basically what is being muted here is; the bollockese employed by individuals to hype Mr Twobly's simplistic scribbles as great art, is verbal /written 'con-artistry'. And my advice to anyone out there that can't see these works for what they really are is to contact www.specsavers.com at the earliest opportunity.

Joe's Quote of Note for Cy Twombly and his scribbles: *"Drawing is the honesty of the art. There is no possibility of cheating; it's either good or bad."* **Salvador Dali**

CHAPTER 13

ROBERT MORRIS

Robert Morris is an American sculptor, conceptual artist and writer. He is regarded as one of the most prominent theorists of Minimalism along with Donald Judd but he has also made important contributions to the development of performance art, minimalism, land art, the Process Art movement and Installation Art.

Born: 9 February 1931, Kansas City, Missouri, United States
Education: Hunter College (1961–1963), more
Periods: Contemporary art, Minimalism
Awards: Guggenheim Fellowship for Creative Arts, US & Canada
Source: Wikipedia

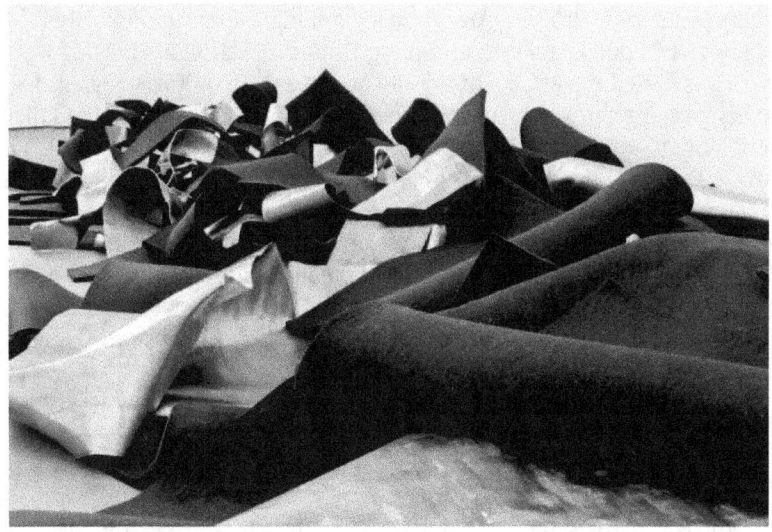

Image@weebly.com

Robert Morris – 'Ms. Edwards' Art Class'
700 × 466 - Lead and Felt (Minimalist Installation)

Part of the Robert Morris Lead & Felt Exhibition
Shown in Major Galleries from the late 1960's

EXAMPLES of ART- BOLLOCKESE*:-

Comments from 'Art Experts' re. The Work's of ROBERT MORRIS:

Extract from www.guggenheim.org re. Robert Morris :

"…During the 1960s and 1970s…Morris explored more elaborate industrial processes for his Minimalist sculpture, using materials such as aluminium and steel mesh. Like these industrial fabrications, a series of Neo-Dada sculptures Morris created in the 1960s also challenged the myth of artistic self-expression. These included ironic "self-portraits" consisting of sculpted brains and electroencephalogram readouts as well as other works directly inspired by Marcel Duchamp's quasi-scientific investigations of perception and measurement.

In the late 1960s and 1970s, the rigid plywood and steel of Morris's Minimalist works gave way to the soft materials of his experiments with Process Art. Primary among these materials was felt, which Morris piled, stacked, and hung from the wall in a series of works that investigated the effects of gravity and stress on ordinary materials. A variety of these felt works were shown in 1968 at the Leo Castelli Gallery, New York. Subsequent projects Morris made during the late 1960s and early 1970s include indoor installations of such unorthodox materials as dirt and thread waste, which resisted deliberate shaping into predetermined forms, and monumental outdoor Earthworks. Since the 1970s, Morris has explored such varied mediums as blindfolded drawings, mirror installations, encaustic paintings, and plaster and fibreglass castings, and themes ranging from nuclear holocaust to Ludwig Wittgenstein's *Philosophical Investigations*…."

Extract from www.widewalls.ch re. Robert Morris

"…Morris's early sculpture tended to emphasize a banal repertoire of form and subject-matter, while attempting to investigate the role of language in artistic representation. Through an influential series of articles that began to appear, irregularly, in the New York art press c. 1966, Morris assumed a highly visible position in determining

---

* **BOLLOCKESE** - Nonsensical verbiage or high-brow language used to communicate; unproven or biased opinion or an exaggerated truth; by a person who possesses or has pretensions of superior learning to project or promote items or concepts.

both the objectives and the tenor of Minimalism in America, then in its early stages…..

….In the late 1960s, Morris began introducing indeterminacy and temporality into the artistic process, referred to as Process art or Anti-Form. By cutting, dropping, or stacking everyday materials such as felt or rags, Morris emphasized the ephemeral nature of the artwork, which would ultimately change every time it was installed in a new space. This replaced what Morris posited as the fixed, static nature of Minimalist, or "object-type," art…."

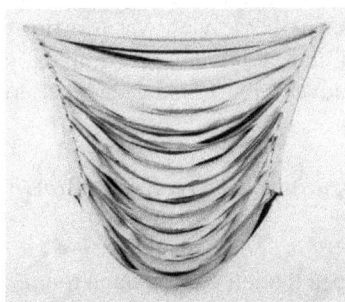

Untitled. Work - 740 × 612
(Material Hanging) By Robert Morris

Part of a Robert Morris collection
shown at the Walker Art Center (USA)

Image@pinterest.com

Extract from www.nytimes.com - re. Robert Morris Jan 12, 2001:

"…Robert Morris's Minimalist sculptures of the 1960's secured him a permanent niche in the history of 20th-century art. But unlike others associated with the path of radical simplification, like Carl Andre, Donald Judd or Dan Flavin, Mr. Morris went on to explore a bewildering variety of other approaches, from scatter art and performance art to representational paintings and sculptures that were allegories of nuclear holocausts.

Detractors, noting Mr. Morris's tendency to pick up ideas from other artists, have questioned his originality and authenticity; supporters see in him a mind too restlessly alive to the possibilities of art to be confined to any one style. This exhibition poses a condensed version of the Morris problem: if you didn't know better, you could easily mistake it for a three-person show.

An otherwise empty room contains a Minimalist work from 1966, a symmetrical arrangement of four pale gray fiberglass platforms. Elsewhere two large wall hangings of thick felt from 1996 recycle ideas about folding and draping that Mr. Morris introduced in the late 1960's; they also call to mind Joseph Beuys's use of felt.

A third room presents works of lead, including three massive panels from 1987, 1988 and 1990. Bearing block-lettered words like "Malice and Doubt" on one piece and "Memoria" on another, they suggest Jasper Johns on steroids.

Contemplating these various directions, one is hard pressed to discover a personal vision connecting them; they are like generic essays on the possibilities of contemporary style. Whether to view Mr. Morris as a clever, opportunistic imitator of himself and others or as a continually interesting aesthetic and philosophical adventurer remains subject to debate…"

Extract taken from www.artinamericamagazine.com - re. Robert Morris. May 01, 2010 :

" In the current exhibition, Morris has heaped the felt pieces in the room's corners and distributed the clean, beautifully crafted metal parts over the polished dark wood floor. A number of the metal pieces also lean against the walls and radiator. In the 1969 installation, the felt and metal mingled together in the rougher brick and concrete warehouse space, both on the floor and against the walls. Although the artist directed the arrangement of the elements of *Untitled (Scatter Piece)* in all its incarnations, he says that his hand is not necessary….

… Morris has always been an intellectually formidable and radical provocateur with a foundation in philosophy (his writings are dense but persuasive) as well as in theater and dance. Even his ostensibly Minimalist sculptures of the mid-'60s relate to performance and movement. Morris's early task-oriented dance work with Simone Forti, Yvonne Rainer, Carolee Schneemann and others shows itself in many of his sculptures, but especially in Post-Minimalist works such as *Untitled (Scatter Piece)* and *Continuous Project Altered Daily*. In both sculptures, workmanlike activity—at the points of inception and installation in the former and on a daily basis in the latter—took precedence over final form….

Morris writes:

"The focus on matter and gravity as means results in forms that were not projected in advance. Considerations of ordering are necessarily casual and imprecise and unemphasized. Random piling, loose stacking, hanging, give passing form to the material. Chance is accepted and indeterminacy is implied, as replacing will result in another configuration. Disengagement with preconceived enduring forms is a positive assertion. It is part of the work's refusal to continue estheticizing the form by dealing with it as a prescribed"... "

 JOE C.THREWITT re. The Work's of ROBERT MORRIS:

Every time this chap Robert Morris walks into 'Carpet Right' they probably shout, "Bingo!.. we haven't got to go to the municipal dump this week with the off-cuts". You therefore have to ask yourself why the hell are people paying to go and see an exhibition of material off-cuts scattered randomly across a gallery? Just take a-peek inside your garage or shed. If it's anything like mine, you will have your own gallery exhibition right on your door-step, if its random dross you want to look at.

As with the majority of these exhibits, the self-appointed art-know-alls have named such random scattering of items; 'concept art'. This includes anything strewn across the floor or up the wall and in keeping with this modern acceptance of what is now determined as Art, there appears to be no requirement for creative skill. So why are we letting ourselves be constantly conned that this is 'Art', even if it is blatantly contrary to the English language meaning of the word?   Also, it is understood Mr Morris himself has seemingly questioned this.

This is recorded in some of the bollockese written about Robert Morris and his own underlying feelings about his works: *"...the artist directed the arrangement of the elements of Untitled (Scatter Piece) in all its incarnations, he says that his hand is not necessary: in fact he told the gallery director, Barbara Castelli, that she could do it herself, and when she demurred, he suggested, perhaps humorously, or perhaps not, that she could ask a couple of eight-year-olds to take on the task."*

It has also been quoted (www.widewalls.ch/Milja Ficpatrik); *"..That when a collector, the architect Philip Johnson, did not pay Morris for a work he had ostensibly purchased, the artist drew up a certificate of de-authorization that officially withdrew all aesthetic content from his piece, making it nonexistent as art."*

Accordingly it appears Mr Morris has certified his work not to be Art and furthermore has claimed it could be done by any child. Therefore the man has seemingly done the right thing and described his work for what it is; randomly strew rubbish. Not Art. Whether these comments were made tongue-in-cheek or in recognition of the truth? Who knows! Well actually we all do if we're honest, with the latter winning every-time.

Although Robert Morris is known predominantly for his minimalist sculptured efforts, he has also created pictorial works in an architectural style. These are pretty damn good. Take a look at his 'Tower of Silence' and other similar pieces. These works certainly display some technical skill, albeit in most architects' offices you can find works as good and probably more elaborate. Although this again raises the question; what is Art and what should be determined as artworks aligned to items created by other recognised professions or by an industry in which they hold a functional use?

Nevertheless, given that Mr Morris does possess artistic technical skill, why does he bother with the conceptual pieces described, that are just bits-and-bobs scattered or drooped against walls. The truth of course lies behind why minimalism was truly introduced as an art form. Minimalism in art has been determined by the art-boffs to mean; *"Abstract painting or sculpture in which expressiveness and illusion are minimized by the use of simple geometric shapes, flat colour, and arrangements of ordinary objects (Source British Dictionary)"*

However, if you ever hear of a minimalist art exhibition of any kind, you can guarantee it will be full of inane flotsam and jetsam or absolutely nothing. Minimalism is definitely one of those made up art 'isms' that are nothing more than an excuse to market works containing little or no skill, with Mr Morris not wishing to miss the trick, jumping on this sad bandwagon. There is no doubt Mr Morris like many of his conceptual *non*-creative pals are clever individuals. The truth is most of us would love to have notoriety and / or wealth for doing the least possible. So, when these clever *con*-artists established the term 'minimalist conceptual art' and gained acceptance and often great praise from the art-elite…They certainly cracked it! And yes of course most of us are envious. This is because we all know we could easily create the absurd bunkum being exhibited. That is if we were given the time, money and support of the art-bollockese merchants allied to these so-called art-works. Imagine just tossing a few bits and bobs around the room and then being paid good money and even receiving praise for it. Totally bonkers but… Marvellous!

Although we may recognise these works as being 'nuckin futs', the bollockese spouted from the art-intellectuals seems to have successfully convinced gallery owners otherwise. However, the truth probably is; the gallery owners love this conceptual inane stuff because the job of the curator displaying the fatuous collection is simply very simple. They can just lob it all in a pile wherever they like as it just doesn't make any odds. Therefore it requires little or no skill on their part and little or no skill by the exhibitor. For them it's just a win win!

This is why Joe Public should wise-up. Just ignore the bollockese and see the minimalist bundle of garbage for the rubbish it really is. Only then will we ensure we get our money's worth out of these shysters. Alternatively, roll over, pay-up and take it on board that such minimalist works are as the bollockese claims; "…*challenging the myth of artistic self expression….attempting to investigate the role of language in artistic representation* … or simply… *introducing indeterminacy and temporality into the artistic process.. of Anti-Form."*

These so-called intellectuals know if they can make you believe in '*isms*' and '*Anti-Forms*' you're believe anything and the fact some do beggars belief!

Joe's Quote of Note for Mr Morris and his off-cut drapes and clutter:
   " Lack of skill dictates economy in style." **Joey Ramone**

CHAPTER 14

BARNETT NEWMAN

Barnett Newman (January 29, 1905 – July 4, 1970) was an American artist. He is seen as one of the major figures in abstract expressionism and one of the foremost of the colour field painters. His paintings are existential in tone and content, explicitly composed with the intention of communicating a sense of locality, presence, and contingency.

Image @ sotherbys.com

Barnett Newman - ONEMENT VI

Signed and dated *1953* in dark blue paint on lower right corner
Oil on canvas
102 x 120 in. 259.1 x 304.8 cm

Sold for $43.8 Million
Sotherby's New York in 2013

EXAMPLES of ART- BOLLOCKESE*:-

Comments from 'Art Experts' re. The Work's of BARNET NEWMAN:

Extract taken from www.theguardian.com column Thursday 16th May *2013:*

" Barnett Newman is well worth $43.8m. Great art is essentially priceless. The highest price paid by the most well-heeled collector is only a fraction of its true value.

And Newman is a great artist.

The price put on greatness at Sotheby's in New York this week, where works by Francis Bacon and Jeff Koons failed to sell but Newman soared, is the $43.8m paid for his Onement VI.

If you are going to buy a Newman, this is the kind of Newman you should buy: a powerful example of his ineffable style at its height of confidence and magic.

A single white line divides a flat expanse of blue: it seems to rip open the universe, a crack in space and time. Versions of this vertical line appear again and again in Newman's paintings, sometimes alone as in his 1946 work Moment in Tate Modern, sometimes in a series of vertical parallels, like mappings of energy pulses or avant garde musical notation – witness his masterpiece Vir Heroicus Sublimis which hangs in New York's Museum of Modern Art.

Standing in front of Vir Heroicus Sublimis – "man heroic and sublime" – you feel the excitement and audacity of the boldest of America's abstract expressionist painters.

After the second world war, as the US became a superpower, a new generation of artists made New York the centre of modern art, with a strange yet authoritative form of abstraction that was free from the influence of the still-living European modern masters. Abstract expressionism uses spacious surfaces, covering wall-scaled canvases with

---

* **BOLLOCKESE** - Nonsensical verbiage or high-brow language used to communicate; unproven or biased opinion or an exaggerated truth; by a person who possesses or has pretensions of superior learning to project or promote items or concepts.

flowing expanses of colour that embrace the spectator. Jackson Pollock broke the ice for this new American painting, but Newman gave it the simplest, starkest formulation.

Meaning and dream collide hypnotically in his art. His vertical line, full of portent (but not "portentous", as sceptics might claim) speaks of creation, God – and the human urge to draw a line. Yet this primeval mark slices through entrancing colour that draws you in at a deep psychic level, irrationally, like falling into deep water.

Newman's universe is primitive, yet utterly modern. In Manhattan the grandeur of Vir Heroicus Sublimis mirrors the skyscrapers looming all around. He saw himself as a political artist and one of his most poignant works can be found in front of the Rothko Chapel in Houston, Texas. It is a massive sculpture called Broken Obelisk; the line that connects Earth and heaven has been cut.

It stands in Houston as a monument to Martin Luther King. Newman said he hoped it offered "a glimpse of the sublime". His art embodies the immense ambition of the US, its fault lines and tragedies. Yet it is more than American. It expresses the universal human impulse to find meaning in the void…"

Extract from www.sothebys.com catalogue note *14 May 2013 - 13 May 2013 - New York* :

"…..Newman concisely memorialized his commitment to pure painting as a totality of transcendence, devoid of subject matter aside from the belief in the visual and spiritual phenomena of his creations so beautifully embodied by *Onement VI* of 1953. Newman recognized that his aesthetic ideas had been at last given form and his own unique pictorial language had been realized. Aided by his move to a larger studio at 110 Watt Street in August 1950, Newman's paintings expanded in scale as the grounds, voids, rhythms and zips spill beyond the edges of his canvas to encompass the viewer in a spiritual dialogue.

The ambitious size of paintings such as *Onement VI*, which at the time was not accommodating for most homes or even galleries, was not however related simply to mere measurements or illusionistic depth, as Ann Temkin observed in her essay for the 2002 retrospective of Newman's work in Philadelphia: "Newman, however, always talked in terms of scale, not size….Newman's paintings prove that the dynamics on which they depend for success could operate on very little surface.

What counted was the emotional resonance – the perfect adjustment of a color and the size and shape of its extent and to what neighbored it.".....

... With its title, *Onement VI* honors Newman's quest for the totality of the art object, evoking emotional and spiritual resonance with essential and organic features. Newman's aesthetic philosophy was expressed in his greatest essay on abstract art, "The Plasmic Image", which was published posthumously. In this lengthy treatise, Newman outlined the search for a universal art and defined abstract forms as 'plasmic' – which he identified with an organic fluidity like the movement of thoughts as opposed to the 'plastic' of inert matter like paint or marble.

As Newman elaborated, "The new painter feels that these (abstract shapes) must contain the plasmic entity that will carry his thought, the nucleus that will give life to the abstract, even abstruse ideas he is projecting. ...The effect of these new pictures is that the shapes and colors act as symbols to (elicit) sympathetic participation on the part of the beholder in the artist's vision." (John P. O'Neill, *Op. Cit.,* pp. 141-142)

In *Onement VI*, the single zip resonates within the canvas and with the viewer; it is described both by sharp tactile edges that retain a crisp memory of the delineating tape and by the gentle laps of marine blue that seep into the void of the cool light blue. Soft ghostly traces toward the bottom of the zip disperse as if into air, while deeper bleeds at eye level seek to bridge the gap of the zip from edge to edge, creating a spatial tension. The act of the pigment bleed is the locus of the temporal element in Newman's work that finds corresponding resonance with the temporal experience of viewing *Onement VI* at our leisure and contemplatively.

As Harold Rosenberg wrote in his 1978 monograph on Newman, "The format of *Onement I* takes its meaning from being experienced as an undifferentiated whole, thus functioning as a 'space vehicle' for the idea of singularity. Oneness itself in Newman's terms is an exalted 'subject matter'." (Harold Rosenberg, Barnett Newman, New York, 1978, pp. 59-60) As the agent of inner coherence to the painting, the zip of *Onement VI* is also the agent of identity and universality, brought so memorably to life in the sculptures in zip form, such as *Here I (To Marcia)* of 1950/1962, so named when Marcia Weisman, the purchaser of *Onement VI* in 1961, prevailed on Newman to cast a 1962 bronze based on a 1950 plaster and wood construction. Placed prominently in the Weisman's collection, Newman's painting and sculpture gave graphic testimony to the enduring power of Newman's creations.

Critics who were puzzled at Newman's work in the early 1950s sometimes regarded his paintings as philosophic statements made without artistic attributes, or conversely, as pure painting devoid of a subject. Paintings such as *Onement VI*, in truth, involve both spirit and nature, and Newman sought to instill in the viewer a profound sense of the spiritual. This did not imply that Newman was religious, but rather that he sought a profound faith in the role of the artist in attaining the highest realm to which a man could aspire. For Newman, art was capable of provoking in the viewer an existential sense of awe and wonderment for the sublime miracle of existence..."

 JOE C.THREWITT re. The Work's of BARNET NEWMAN:

Having looked into this art history malarkey, it seems apparent the rot set in sometime in the 1950's. Some would argue it all kicked-off in 1874, when a group of artists called the Anonymous Society of Painters, Sculptors, Printmakers, etc. organized an exhibition in Paris that launched the movement called Impressionism. Its founding members included Claude Monet, Edgar Degas, and Camille Pissarro, among others. Nevertheless, although it would appear there was a dumbing-down in pictorial detail, there was still pictorial excellence, albeit, the subject matter may have taken on a wafty appearance. The overall picture and colour build up of these early impressionists really do show some skill in application and is there for all to see.

However, contrary to the gushing bollockese you read, one could argue it really is the likes of Barnet and his fellow art simpletons who should be blamed for dragging Art down to the depths of it's simplistic despair of today. This of course assisted by the descriptive fraudulent bollockese that claims *'abstract impressionism'* is anything other than a picture that could be randomly created by anyone, or anything, that can apply paint to a surface.

Unlike some of Mr Newman's contemporaries who paint blocks of colour and call them Art, at least he makes an effort and puts in the odd stripe or two. However, of common knowledge to an accomplished artists is; when you paint stripes, the use of masking-tape is a good thing if you want to produce a straight edge. The average Joe also knows if you use most types of masking-tape on a rough surface it bleeds under the tape and looks bloody awful.

So tell me, if Mr Newman is the "*..great artist..*" as one of the above art intellectual commentators claim, we can reasonably assume with some surety he knows his stuff about paint and painting. However, having looked closer at his $43.8 Million Onement VI pic, it appears he has painted the canvas an attractive blue with oil paint over a strip of masking tape down the middle. It also seems clear when he pulled off the masking-tape it has bled ..go on take a look!. Therefore in my summation this so called great artist deserves about 1/10 for the effort and probably less for technical ability.

Enough of this pedantic criticism; you can't beat about the bush with so-called Art like this. Without the accompanying bollockese, it is exactly what you see. Mr Barnett's Onement VI picture appears to be a simplistic poorly executed piece of work that Joe C. Threwitt reckons anyone with an amoebic cell could produce and now do in their droves. What also is equally absurd is the bollockese guff written about these blocks of colour; often referred to as, "Exquisite examples of *minimalist* or *abstract impressionist* works".. What!...Open your eyes what do you really see?

However, let's try and be a bit positive here. As previously mentioned it's not good to speak ill of people who are no longer with us. And let's face it; Mr Newman is not solely responsible for his dubious success. The art-intellectual bollockese written about all these simplistic works involving little or no skill that have afforded such undeserved notoriety, are really the issue here. Mr Newman like many others, just ride the bollockese wave and in doing so has made a tidy living for themselves with little effort afforded to their productions. Nevertheless, I am still struggling to find something positive here...Okay say you were to put a collection of Mr Newman's coloured blocks together they would probably make an excellent pin-board for a primary school wall...There you go!

Anyhow let's leave the creation of these kinder-garden blocks of colour to one side and look at the bollockese tosh acclaiming hyped praise on these works. These art-bollockese chappies have the gall to claim the simplistic blocks of colour with a line down the middle express:

"*...a powerful example of his ineffable style at its height of confidence and magic.*"

"...Meaning and dream collide hypnotically.... His vertical line, full of portent (but not "portentous", as sceptics might claim) speaks of creation, God – and the human urge to draw a line. Yet this primeval mark slices through entrancing colour that draws you in at a deep psychic level, irrationally, like falling into deep water."

"..the single zip resonates within the canvas and with the viewer; it is described both by sharp tactile edges that retain a crisp memory of the delineating tape and by the gentle laps of marine blue that seep into the void of the cool light blue. Soft ghostly traces toward the bottom of the zip disperse as if into air, while deeper bleeds at eye level seek to bridge the gap of the zip from edge to edge, creating a spatial tension. The act of the pigment bleed is the locus of the temporal element in Newman's work that finds corresponding resonance."

What are these people on!

These being prime examples of the 'descriptive fraud' used so prevalently in the current art world... It really does make a reasonable man want to throw-up.

Seemingly even more bizarre; someone has taken on-board all this bollockese bunkum and paid good money to the sum of $43.8 Million for something that if I paid more than a tenner for, I'd feel robbed.... No! I don't think I'd even pay a tenner.

The wasters who pay absurd amounts for such artworks, could build fully equipped hospitals or schools, or fund over a thousand nurses or teachers for a year!.. But for some reason, which probably involves the hope of making even more money to waste, he or she chooses to believe some ridiculous intellectual bollockese and purchases a coloured-block anyone with digits and a pot of paint could create. No doubt such individuals feel like knowledgeable Art collectors. It surely can't be because these artworks looks good or exhume quality.. Because they just don't!

Wouldn't you just love it if the genuine Arty people re-looked at simplistic efforts like this and take on board some common sense and reviewed these works for what they really are, with a worth of no more than the canvas they adorn. As old Bill Shakespeare would say, *"There's no legacy so rich as honesty"* and to make these work worthless, as they should be, would possibly go some way to make some crazy rich collector grow some badly needed sense of reality. He may then put his money into investments that would at least provide a legacy with an element of true value…or maybe not!

The intellectual and the rich may argue to the contrary spouting their bollockese, but truly there is no other tangible item showing less effort for bizarre reward than *minimalist* and *abstract impressionist* works like Mr Newman's and his mates so called Art. Think about it, then tell me I'm wrong… You just can't!

Joe's Quote of Note for Mr Newman and other minimalists:
"There's a fine line between minimalism and not trying very hard"
Tom Pappalardo

CHAPTER 15

HENRY FLYNT
(Not to be confused with Henry Flint)

Henry Flynt (born 1940 in Greensboro, North Carolina) is a philosopher, avant-garde musician, anti-art activist and exhibited artist often associated with Conceptual Art, Fluxus and Nihilism.

In 1961 Flynt coined the term **concept art** in the Neo-Dada, proto-Fluxus book *An Anthology of Chance Operations* (co-published by Jackson Mac Low and La Monte Young) that was released in 1963. *An Anthology of Chance Operations* contained seminal works by Fluxus artists such as George Brecht and Dick Higgins. Flynt's *concept art*, he maintained, devolved from cognitive nihilism, from insights about the vulnerabilities of logic and mathematics. *Source Wikapdia.*

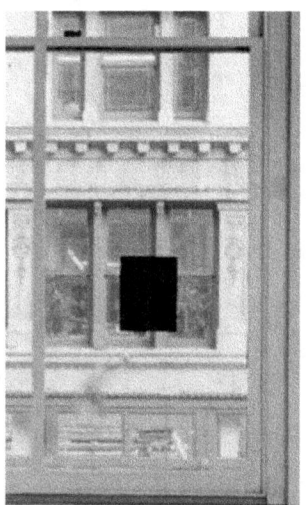

Image @ henryflynt.org

Henry Flynt – Interior Boundary Painting (1992 Installation):

A mask on a black square, which was installed on a windowpane in the Kunstverein's upstairs foyer – looking through the window revealed shifting visual information depending on viewers' perspectives – the frame surrounding the image (and hence the piece) perpetually fluid

EXAMPLES of ART- BOLLOCKESE*:-

Comments from 'Art Experts' re. The Work's of HENRY FLYNT:

Extract from: www.frieze.com/article/henry-flynt 13 Feb 2013 :

"....The sole purpose of this argument is to cause trouble', begins Henry Flynt's ambitiously titled 1997 treatise *That 1 = 2*. Systematic provocation might also have been the goal of Activities 1959–, this retrospective and first-ever institutional exhibition by the US artist / anti-artist / musician / philosopher. Curated by Kunstverein director Hans-Jürgen Hafner in close collaboration with Flynt, the show brought together visual pieces, some of them recreations of previous versions, which unfolded and collapsed in contradiction, as well as the artist's unique brand of very reasoned nonsense.

Flynt's prints and paintings comprise diagrammatic illusions, semantic puzzles and optical quandaries which seem clipped from Logic or Gestalt psychology textbooks. The intermedial hand of Fluxus is never too far, though Flynt disputes the association (despite his friendship with La Monte Young, George Maciunas and Tony Conrad). This distancing seems to be part of his attempt to stake out ground for his work on its own terms, in conceptual solitude. Likewise, as acts of crystalline optical reduction, these pieces strip visual experience to the rudiments of viewership. *Interior Boundary Painting* (1992), for example, is a mask on a black square, which was installed on a windowpane in the Kunstverein's upstairs foyer – looking through the window revealed shifting visual information depending on viewers' perspectives – the frame surrounding the image (and hence the piece) perpetually fluid.....

...... *Logically Impossible Space*, first realized at the 1990 Venice Biennale, features an empty room whose walls are printed with dozens of Necker cubes: an optical illusion wherein the brain, in perceiving a two-dimensional figure as a three-dimensional cube, sees the 'front' of the cube as the 'back', and vice versa. The effect of multidirectional illusion was compounded by the number of Neckers, as well as this piece's installation in a cubic space opposite the Kunstverein...."

---

* **BOLLOCKESE** - Nonsensical verbiage or high-brow language used to communicate; unproven or biased opinion or an exaggerated truth; by a person who possesses or has pretensions of superior learning to project or promote items or concepts.

Extract from: www.cairn.info/revue-le-philosophoire-2006. - "For an Acognitive Culture: Henry Flynt 's Art Fluxus" :

"....Flynt elaborates his idea of a-cognitive culture within the Fluxus movement. This movement includes artists with a different spirit, such as George Maciunas, Dick Higgins, George Brecht, Yoko Ono, Monte Young, Robert Filliou, Ben Vautier and others. The founding principle of the Fluxus practice is the idea of a "permanent flow between art and life". The Latin etymology of the term *fluxus* refers to the idea of incessant passage and flow. Hence the relationship between art and life is cyclical and continual, without interruptions of any kind. It is easy to understand that Fluxus can only refuse the principle of artistic creation, to prefer inactivity. Robert Filliou calls this paradoxical idea the principle *of permanent creation*: "whatever you think, think *of something* else. Whatever you do, do something else.

The absolute secret of permanent creation is to be without desire, without decision, without choice, conscious of oneself, wide awake, sitting quietly, doing nothing ". Because he disputes the idea of art as a *techne* , Fluxus opens the artistic field to ordinary practices: "everyone is an artist". To this criticism of technicality is a conceptual analysis: the suspension of the technical gesture goes hand in hand with the suspension of the concept. In communication, Fluxus prefers the poetics of insignificance; Knowledge, the dismantling of conceptual and linguistic categories; In the fine arts system, the promotion of confusion between disciplines. If there was a talent that was required to the artist Fluxus it would be to know perfectly devoid of talent. Fluxus is a philosophy of life rather than a simple artistic practice. In direct line with the Socratic teaching - which recognizes in the "knowledge not to know" the highest form of wisdom - the Fluxus activity makes the "not-do-do" its founding principle and pushes art towards Its own limits.

At Fluxus, creation is no longer only comparable to its own abstention but also to its own possibility: creation is immediately assimilated sometimes to non-creation and sometimes to mere possibility-of-creation. Hence what Filliou calls the *principle of equivalence*, which *implies* that a well-made work has as much value as an ill-made work and a work not made at all. The formula is: " *Good Done = Done Done = Not Done* ". The idea is that of a strict equivalence between the model (a work "made"), error and transgression (the correspondent "badly done") and finally the unrealized model and therefore its only concept (the "no fact "). "Do", "do it wrong", "do not do" are three strictly equivalent creative modalities. For Filliou, and for the spirit Fluxus in general, art is in no way limited to material execution Of a finite object, but it contains the desire for total creation: the persistence of desire never permits complete satisfaction.

An extreme view of this idea is visible in Henry Flynt, a little-known figure of the Fluxus group. A musician linked to La Monte Young, Flynt proposes a nihilistic theory of art. He defined himself as both an "anti-art activist and a recognized artist" ... The anti-art position common to Fluxus artists is widened in Flynt to the more general domain of culture and philosophy. For Flynt, the aim of art is to dismantle the conventional structures of thought, of which analytical philosophy and cognitivism appear to him as the most resistant fortresses. The fundamental idea of a critique of philosophical culture and traditional aesthetics is firstly called by Flynt "general acognitive culture", then " *veramiously* " and finally " *brend* "... "General acognitive culture", the other terms ...These terminologies allow Flynt to account for the fundamental ambivalence of his principles. By bringing total amusement to the forefront, he considers the playful activities of life as forms of existence that suspend the power of culture without being counter-cultural gestures. Between cultural domination and its corresponding vindictive form (anti-culture), Flynt prefers the pacification of acognitivism, a kind of cultural state beyond all knowledge.

The idea of a general acognitive culture is for Flynt a way of replacing artistic creation by "recreation", by a practice having as its end mere amusement (the *veramiously*) "My new concept of general acognitive" ...A kind of second and repeated creation, re-creation can only lose the demiurgic and inventive meaning of original creation: recreation produces nothing but itself, which means that it produces nothing of the all. Its purpose is internal and its production simply null. For Flynt, the rejection of cognitivism means at the same time the effacement of the philosophical conceptions already established and the refusal of the art as fabrication of works.

The gestures of acognitive culture are therefore not to be confused with those of manual labor. Brend *activities are* fun for recreation as they provide comfort and relaxation after a more serious activity. Consequently, acognitive culture is also a critique of society, insofar as social activities are linked to productive work. If work is simply a means of achieving other goals (economic stability, social recognition, personal satisfaction, etc.), Acognitive culture is to itself its own end, namely amusement. In the end, "one can not create an acognitive culture as a profession".. "One can not create acognitive culture as a profession ... .

Flynt's anti-art erects our most playful forms of life to the rank of aesthetic practices. Spontaneous play, gestures made solely for pleasure, amusements of body and language become here the matrix of recreation. Hence, acognitivism can not be limited to excluding the serious structures of thought and art, but must also erase all the notions that arise from it and which could at first sight be related to the so-called ' Creative '. The practice of artistic creation is therefore criticized because it sustains the system of artisanal production. For Flynt, traditional art fails to yield to impersonal canons that move away from individual subjectivity and subject works to abstract notions of pleasure. Through the principal refusal of creation, Flynt joins the idea of permanent creation of Filliou: both distinguish Fluxus art from both mechanical labor and creative work. But if Flynt's ac-culitive culture is a criticism of the notion of work, this does not mean that creation is to be abolished, but rather to reorient. Instead of aiming at the production of an object or the attainment of collective satisfaction, the creation here aims at the reconstruction of the subject performing the gestures. Playful recreation thus becomes a true self-creation..."

 JOE C.THREWITT re. The Work's of HENRY FLYNT:

To even begin to understand where this dude Henry Flynt is coming from you would seemingly need a degree in psychology. There is no doubt Mr Flynt is a high brow academic and as such there is buckets of bollockese surrounding his work. Nevertheless, what the bollockese written about his work is apparently trying to portray 'in brief' is; his works encourage audience response (*Cognitivism*) and at the same time involve the viewer to rely on an element of chance to shape the ultimate outcome of the piece (*Fluxus*).

I was now going to try and provide a more in-depth explanation of the two recent art concepts of *cognitivism* and *fluxus,* but as they are really elitist excuses for producing another batch of bizarre pieces of so called Art with little effort..Ill be just adding to the bollockese you've already read that means absolutely..Jack! Therefore its not even worth the bother.

What does seem certain here is Mr Flynt has found a formula to successfully exhibit works that are simple to produce utilizing an intellectual psycho-concept few understand, or even want to! Basically all that's happening here is the obvious fact, that when you move around an object the view changes. So yes…once again we are being intellectually bushwhacked by bollockese descriptions of what surely is just an obvious everyday occurrence.

The so-called Fluxus Art Movement tenet was to dismiss and mock the elitist world of "high art" and to find any way possible to bring art to the masses, much in keeping with the social climate of the 1960s. So they say!

However, what really happened was the arty-farty intellectuals have eaten this concept up, simply because it is perfect for them to feed off because anything claiming to be anti-establishment has no rules or guidelines. This basically means you can write any old-bollockese about bombed works claiming to adopt this concept. Probably because without any idea of what is good or bad, which after all is the mantra of Fluxus art, the outcome being; anything will do, but unfortunately not without a mass of accompanying bollockese. Fluxus has so back-fired by the nerds that established it and their ranting to; "*purge the (art) world of bourgeoisie sickness…*". How wrong they were. Without the plethora of intellectual bollockese coming from the "art-world bourgeoisie" which always accompanies these works, no one would have a scooby-doo what the hell they are about.

Take for example this load of guff:

"..Flynt's prints and paintings comprise diagrammatic illusions, semantic puzzles and optical quandaries which seem clipped from Logic or Gestalt psychology textbooks."

"..Fluxus is a philosophy of life rather than a simple artistic practice. In direct line with the Socratic teaching - which recognizes in the "knowledge not to know" the highest form of wisdom - the Fluxus activity makes the "not-do-do" its founding principle and pushes art towards Its own limits."

Ahhh doesn't just make you wanna scream…shut the f~#* up.!

The truth is the only persons these art academics are fooling is us. The art-world seemingly sucks up this banal descriptive blurb. The fact that these individuals can form an analogy between art and unexplained cognitive behaviour is a gift so easy to exploit. They do this clear in the knowledge that the only persons who could question and counter any of their babbling philosophical bollockese, are other academics whom also speak a thousand words when just three would do…this really is bullshit!

I've just come across this limerick which just about sums it up:

The frequenters of our picture palaces
Have no use for psychoanalysis;
And although Doctor Freud
Is distinctly annoyed
The truth is the analysis is fallacies.

I don't know about fallacies…it should be faeces. The psychoanalysis babble going on here is not just mistaken garbage but absolute tommy-rot. 'Fluxus'… talk about a made up name for a made up nonsensical concept. It would have been more apt if it were called 'Fuxus'!. Nevertheless, Fluxus describes itself as: *"..art produced by a range of artists with a shared sensibility as an attempt to 'fuse... cultural, social, & political revolutionaries into [a] united front and action'* (*Wikapedia*).

In my view the *Wikapedia* description of 'Fluxus' should read; *'An excuse for a form of art for the lazy / or the technically inept'.*

There is no doubt Mr Flynt fancied himself more as a philosopher than an artist. His later works even portray just framed philosophical quotes like, "DEMOLISH SERIOUS CULTURE". This all seems a bit oxymoronic. Simply because the words he exhibits appear to be an attempt to express what he really believes he is; the conveyor of a serious cultural thinking concept.

Therefore, what we have here is a mass of bollockese surrounding just another form of lazy, crazy and banal works determined as a new art-concept. So, summing up; if you put all these works together in an exhibition together with all the intellectual bollockese written about them, yes you could easy fill a gallery. However if you ask for an explanation of what it's all about… it's guaranteed your be bored senseless within minutes of being drowned in bollockese. This is simply because in reality the so-called conceptual art of Fluxus is exactly what you see and read about it… crap wrapped in intellectual toilet-paper!

Joe's Quote of Note for Mr Flynt and his Fluxus inventions:
"...Invention in my opinion arises from idleness, possibly also from laziness to save oneself trouble." **Agatha Christie**

CHAPTER 16

FRANZ KLINE

Franz Kline was an American painter born in Pennsylvania. He is mainly associated with the Abstract Expressionist movement of the 1940s and 1950s.

Born: 23 May 1910, Wilkes-Barre, Pennsylvania, United States
Died: 13 May 1962, New York City, New York, United States
Periods: Modern art, Action painting, Abstract expressionism
Parents: Anthony Kline, Anne Kline
Education: Girard College, Boston University.
Source Wikapdia

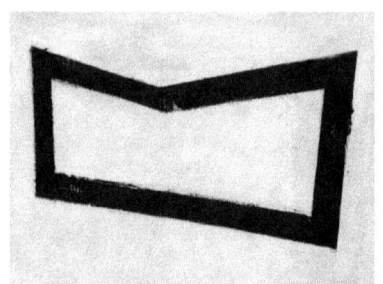

Images @ Guggenheim.org

FRANZ KLINE – Untitled (1950's)
Oil on canvas

FRANZ KLINE – Painting No.7 (1952)
Oil on canvas

EXAMPLES of ART- BOLLOCKESE*:-

Comments from 'Art Experts' re. The Work's of FRANZ KLINE:

Extract from: www.guggenheim.org:

"Throughout the 1940s, while many artists of the nascent New York School were experimenting with Surrealist-inspired biomorphic abstraction, Franz Kline was painting landscapes and portraits. Consequently, in 1950, when the artist showed large, gestural abstract paintings in his first solo exhibition, it appeared that he had experienced a wholesale conversion. Much has been made of a 1949 visit he paid to his friend Willem de Kooning, who asked Kline for some of the drawings he always carried in his pockets and projected them onto the wall, monumentalizing details of the sketches. While this episode may have been a catalyst for Kline's mature style, by the end of the 1940s his work was already yielding to a looser application of paint and a more emphatic expressionistic technique.

Kline scored his success in the early 1950s with large canvases onto which he applied black and white commercial paint with housepainter's brushes. He became known as an Action painter because his work expressed movement and energy, emphasizing dynamic line. The characteristic black slashes of *Painting No. 7* suggest the full body movement of the artist as he spontaneously applied the paint, incorporating chance splatters and smearing. In fact, Kline's paintings were constructed only to look as if they were painted in a moment of inspiration—they usually resulted from the transfer of a sketch to the canvas.

Unlike de Kooning and Jackson Pollock, Kline never flirted with figuration in his abstract paintings and avoided spatial ambiguity. *Painting No. 7* is among the artist's most straightforward statements; it also demonstrates his knowledge of art history. Kline's emphasis on the square in this and other works suggests his interest in Josef Albers and Kazimir Malevich. Art historian Harry Gaugh cites Piet Mondrian's *Composition No. 1: Lozenge with Four Lines* (1930) as an influence, and

---

* **BOLLOCKESE** - Nonsensical verbiage or high-brow language used to communicate; unproven or biased opinion or an exaggerated truth; by a person who possesses or has pretensions of superior learning to project or promote items or concepts.

also contends that the compositional structure of *Painting No. 7* recalls James McNeill Whistler's *Arrangement in Gray and Black, No. 1* (1871). Though the similarity between the latter two paintings might appear incidental, Kline referred to Whistler in other paintings, and the austere geometry of Whistler's canvas would have appealed to him.
Jennifer Blessing…"

Extract from: www.gagosian.com :

" Franz Kline used stark tonal contrasts and variations of scale to explore gestural movement in his Abstract Expressionist paintings. The early abstract work of friend and colleague Willem de Kooning had a deep impact on Kline, who began working as a painter in New York in the late 1930s. Moving away from figurative representation, Kline experimented with projecting small, abstract ink sketches onto his studio wall, enlarging nuanced brush strokes to mural-sized cyphers. These early exercises would inspire the large, black-and-white gestural paintings that became Kline's legacy. He developed a painting practice that rejected many conventions of the medium: working at night under harsh lighting to bring out the tonal play between black and white and applying both oil and enamel with house-painting brushes created textural inconsistencies and left a record of the artist's movement. Though contemporary critics often credited the influence of Japanese calligraphy (a reading that the artist consistently denied), the sweeping vectors that dominate Kline's thickly painted canvases convey the emotion embedded in the act of painting itself…."

Extract from: www.independent.co.uk – "Art / The master builder: Franz Kline" *Monday 11 July 1994* :

"…Kline makes no attempt to conjure the transcendentally charged voids of Rothko. He is equally uninterested in the cosmic metaphorical possibilities of abstract painterly gesture which so preoccupied Jackson Pollock. His is an art charged with a dark, heavy, sullen materiality: an art of and for the city, New York, that was both his adopted home - he had been born, in 1910, in a steel town in Pennsylvania - and his most enduring theme. Kline was not perhaps, in the end, as great an artist as either Pollock or Rothko, but he was a considerable one, and the time is right to rescue his work from the relative oblivion to which art history has, in recent years, consigned it….."

.....Kline's paintings, like all paintings and most especially like all New York School paintings, are thoroughly denatured by reproduction. In reproduction, their scale, which is so important to their effects, is entirely lost. But so, too, is the sometimes subtle heaviness and the constant hesitancy of Kline's handling. The comparison that has frequently been drawn between his brushstrokes and the free, loose spontaneity of oriental calligraphy is convincing only superficially and only when his pictures are seen in reproduction. In reality, the marks that Kline made on his canvases, applied with thick housepainter's brushes, are anything but spontaneous. His pictures are slow, not fast: things that have been painstakingly constructed, not conceived in the mind's eye and executed with the swiftness of thought. The heaviness of Kline's black girders and joists and I-beams, built in layers and then feathered into white pictorial voids, gives his pictures their most powerful quality, which is fundamentally architectural. Kline paints a picture with something of the stubborn, improvisational character of an amateur carpenter building a house.

This heavy, built quality in Kline's painting has made him one of the unacknowledged heroes of what might be termed a distinctively American blue-collar aesthetic: an aesthetic which, although it has tended to produce works of art commonly referred to as abstract, is much more interested in realities than abstractions. Kline's dark blocks of paint, his scaffolding traceries, his asphalt highways - these link him, not to Pollock or Rothko, but more closely to a tradition of constructed American sculpture initiated by David Smith and continued today, albeit in a very different vein, by Richard Serra, whose huge constructions of rusting sheet-steel, full of a distinctly American sense of the grandeur of American heavy industry, often look like Klines made solid and three-dimensional.

Franz Kline
Meryon
1960–1

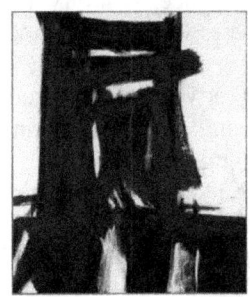

Image @theartstack.com

Although Kline's pictures are abstract they are shot through with a powerful sense of place and, at their best, they look like stunned memories of those towering monuments that are the bridges and skyscrapers of New York. Palladio, with its huge heavy black forms rushed into indistinctness by some of Kline's most flurried, excited painting, is like a recollection of New York as seen from a speeding car or through the windows of an elevated train. There may be a kind of jingoism behind that title: Kline's way of saying that the old architectural innovativeness of Europe, embodied in the buildings produced by that ancient tradition inherited and passed on by Palladio, has migrated to America. Meryon, the most impressive of all the pictures in the Whitechapel exhibition, is the Brooklyn Bridge reconfigured, rebuilt in paint and, in the process, reconceived as a symbol: an emblem, in its powerful thrust of great engineered shapes into cloudy whiteness, of nothing less than the vast energies and equally vast aspirations of a new and newly self-confident American nation...."

 JOE C.THREWITT re. The Work's of FRANZ KLINE:

Now I have seen some early works of Franz Kline that are not really bad, in particular his depictions of clowns. He also produced some colourful geometric abstract works that were...err colourful. Then in the 1950's along with some other New York based so-called artists, including the *de Koonings*, he joined a group who became known as 'The New York School'. This group produced works which they termed as *abstract impressionist* and *action works*.
Nevertheless, in the real world this group should have been called 'The New York School of Couch Potato Art' as the works Kline produced as a result of this concept allegiance, contrary to the bollockese and $40 Million dollar price tag, seems woeful to say the least.

The theme is again pretty clear; why produce complex pieces of art work that requires some sense of visual recognition of the subject which inevitably is time consuming, when you can simply wipe a dollop of black paint across a canvas and be afforded great acclaim. The bollockese merchants put Kline's transition from okay to dire as *"..Kline's mature style ... yielding to a looser application of paint and a more emphatic expressionism technique.."*

'Emphatic expressionism technique'...my butt! These bollockese boffs even claim Kline's big black daubs show him to be an "..*action painter*..". No way!

Peter Paul Rubens '*Massacre of the Innocents*' or Joseph Mallord Turners '*Snow Storm- Steam Boat off a Harbour's Mouth*'... now these are true examples of artists that deserve the recognition of being *action painters*.

Not quite understanding how the two everyday words 'action' and 'painting' have been allowed to become synonymous to works that are just random paint daubs or splatters, a bit of research was definitely in order. It appears the term 'action painting' was high-jacked by an American art intellectual named: Harold Rosenberg in 1952, in his essay "The American Action Painters". Why anyone thought this term should become something this dude should claim ownership on behalf of the USA, or have the audacity to award the term to such crappy paintings only god knows. There are so many existing art works that fit the two word English language description far more appropriately, Harry's action painting claims for America certainly beggars belief.

This Yank, who's definitely yanking your chain, claims the following bollockese: *Action painting is a style or type of painting that does not follow a certain pattern or flow. As an art, the paint is basically just splashed or smeared unto the canvas contrary to the other paintings in which the paint is carefully applied thus, creating a certain image of what the artist wants to show. In this aspect, action painting is drawn simultaneously to give a certain effect with which only the viewer can see what it is all about, regardless of what the artist would want to convey. It would only be about of what the perception of the viewer is. If there is however an image depicted in the action painting, it would now be the task of the viewer to see and figure that out.*

This is just another load of art-bollockese dross spewing from a septic-tank! 'Action Paintings' are exactly what the words say... paintings that portray action. They definitely are not limited to a bunch of slap dash New York daubsters.

Although there is a distinct lack of skill required to produce these random swages of paint, it would be wrong to suggest the works are not Art. They are just another example of simpleton art dressed up by art-intellectual bollockese to be something they definitely bloody well aren't...well executed art-works. The boffs here describe Kline depicting architectural structures with his bold black lines.. I'm sorry boffs they are just broad black lines on a white canvas and to those with normal vision and living in this world... they bare no resemblance to any structure on this planet. But maybe they do if you live on planet 'La..La..Land'.

Even more absurd than the architectural analogy of Kline's works is the absolute bollockese mentioned above referring to comments made by Art historian Harry Gaugh whom contended. ". *that the compositional structure of (Kline's) Painting No. 7 recalls James McNeill Whistler's Arrangement in Gray and Black, No. 1 (1871)."*

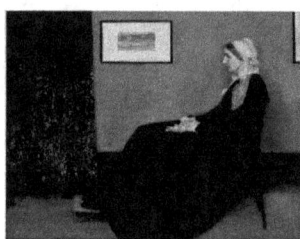

Image@guggenheim.org   Image@wikipedia.org

Errr..I don't think so! Apart from Kline's daubs on the left of the canvas being scrawled about the same place as the curtains depicted in the Whistler painting, Mr Gaugh is just whistling in the wind. To even suggest any comparison between Kline's Painting No.7 and anything created by a true art master like Whistler, just goes to prove the craziness' of the art-bollockese we are dealing with here!

Joe's Quote of Note for Mr Kline and his black slashes: *"Painting is easy when you don't know how, but very difficult when you do."*
Edgar Dagas

CHAPTER 17

STANLEY BROUWN

S tanley Edmund Brouwn (Paramaribo , 25 June 1935) is a Dutch conceptual artist of Surinamese descent.

According to his scant biography, Brouwn came to Amsterdam from Suriname in 1957. His fellow artist friend Armando introduced him to the Zero movement, a group of artists who rejected the evident authorial signature. Brouwn's first works, dating from that time, which he later destroyed, were transparent polythene bags filled with all sorts of rubbish and hung from the ceiling. The work consisted of the visible content of the bag and nothing else. The pieces he actually considers to be his first works were ones he didn't make himself: instead, he laid paper sheets on the street and an unsuspecting cyclist or pedestrian created the art work as they cycled or walked over them. Without realizing it, the passers-by became anonymous partners in these works capturing movement and time. Through participation, Brouwn placed the act of creation into the hands of others and subsequently erased, in a certain sense, his own artisthood.

He made in 1984/85 Work *Project for the Rijksmuseum Kröller-Müller* for Sculpture from the Kröller-Müller Museum in Otterlo , consisting of ten text as signs marking the beginning ten points he walked distances in the sculpture garden. The Kröller-Müller Museum further includes operate an extensive collection of Brouwn.

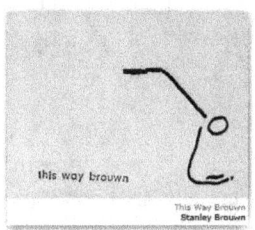

Image@artistbooksandmultiples.co.uk

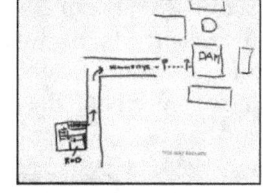

Image@lesartistecontemporains.com

Stanley Brouwn- 'This Way Brouwn" (1964)

A conceptual work in which the artist had a person draw a map leading to the Dam Platz in Amsterdam. Stamped in blue ink LR "THIS WAY BROUWN"

EXAMPLES of ART- BOLLOCKESE:-

*Comments from 'Art Experts' re. The Work's of STANLEY BROUWN:

Extract from: www.lesartistescontemporains.com:

" Since the early 1960s, Stanley Brouwn has refused any personal catalogue containing other indications than the strict description of the works on display. His withdrawal from any public scene... explains in part the discretion in which his work is kept. It is, however, a work based on internal rigor and coherence, which make it one of the most significant works of Conceptual Art .

However, unlike other conceptual artists, Stanley Brouwn is always in relation to a physical reality. Its language is constituted not within a closed field, but always in relation to the world.

After destroying his earlier drawings and paintings, and then working with Fluxus artists, he made his first experiments in Amsterdam in 1959: he laid down sheets of paper on the ground that preserved the trace of the passage of pedestrians. In 1960, he began the series This Way, Brouwn sketches of itinerary sketched by passers-by to whom he asks his way and where he then imposes his stamp.

These sketches do not interpret anything; They describe an activity both physical and mental and inscribe the link that the artist maintains with the space. Long before the American conceptual artists, Stanley Brouwn shows that art can arise from mundane situations, to be a trace of the social exchange that flows from it. The work is no longer a single object with aesthetic qualities imposing its contemplation, but the observation of an activity: the displacement of the body in space.

From 1964, he systematized his method by associating the activity described with the precise counting of the elements that compose it..."

---

* **BOLLOCKESE** - Nonsensical verbiage or high-brow language used to communicate; unproven or biased opinion or an exaggerated truth; by a person who possesses or has pretensions of superior learning to project or promote items or concepts.

Extract from www.macba.cat – "Stanley Brouwn Works 1960-2005":

"…According to Brouwn, the possibilities for vertiginous travel that are offered by means of transport such as aeroplanes, have impoverished our perception of distance and rendered it meaningless. Faced with this, the artist has developed an oeuvre that revolves around a creative epicentre based on measuring systems and all kinds of distances, spaces and routes that can be measured. Brouwn's works emerge from everyday experiences, and seek to create awareness of movement. His seemingly minimal gestures conceal a methodical and obsessive process of documentation of the world around us.

The exhibition included drawings, notes, maps, sketches, models, placards and even the walls, floors and display cabinets of the museum. The covering of distances, the moving from a to b, is one of the most essential, everyday human activities. since 1960 the work of Stanley Brouwn has concentrated on this activity. a retrospective presentation of his work from 1960 to the present… ….

…Brouwn uses his own subjective units of measure (the sb-foot, the sb-ell and the sb-step) and sets these against the universally adopted metric system or other – often obsolete – locally used units of measure. at first brouwn noted these distances in sections of line on paper, or in text and figures on filing cards kept in card index boxes or in notebooks. Since the early nineteen eighties he has also used aluminium sheets and strips as well as wooden or metal volumes. He regards these two and three dimensional forms as measuring instruments. By using these units of measure he among others portrays people, buildings, spaces, walls, and floors.

In Brouwn's work, form and material are dependent on concept. for his exhibition walking through cosmic rays at the städtisches museum in mönchengladbach, Brouwn asked the museum to remove all artworks and leave the spaces empty so that people could experience walking through cosmic rays. at the s.m.a.k. in Ghent in 2001 he portrayed the rooms and walls by noting their measurements on cards while the spaces remained empty.

In other works, Brouwn measures existing buildings and marks their sizes on paper or confronts an existing space with a specific unit of measure. In the museu d'art contemporani de barcelona the walls and floors serve as material for works in the exhibition. The display tables and display cases are based on Brouwn measurements. architectural models of yet-to-be-built buildings, based on the sb-foot, the sb-ell and the sb-step, can also be seen. this summer Brouwn realises his first building in Utrecht, the Netherlands.

The earliest works in the exhibition consist of the series this way Brouwn. Brouwn asks passers-by the way from a to b; the directions are clarified by notes on paper. Sometimes the directions are only verbal and the paper remains blank. Brouwn later stamps "this way brouwn" on the sheets of paper. Other works from that same period are the works of footsteps on paper. While walking, Brouwn lets sheets of paper flutter down onto the pavement and the street. The sheets of paper marked with traces of passers-by en route from a to b are later collected again. At the same time Brouwn also makes suggestions for the covering of distances. One such example is the work from 1962 a walk through a grassfield exactly on the same line a-b; every day during a full year.

In the early seventies Brouwn went to morocco and Algeria via Belgium, France and Spain. each day he carefully noted the number of footsteps he took in each of the countries. the result is the work from march 18 until April 18, 1971, I defined my total number of footsteps each day by means of a handcounter, which comprises an inventory of his steps on little cards. this project is the first in a series of works in which Brouwn notes the distances covered during a certain period in a certain country or city while the total amount of steps in a number of countries are recorded. next to these works in which he actually records distances covered there are works in which he constructs and analyses distances, like those in which the distance of 1 metre is described in relation to distances ranging from 1 km to 1 mm.

The material for a later group of works are the imaginary distances between Brouwn and a certain point or person at a certain moment in time. Imaginary lines or triangles change in length from second to second, depending on the position of those involved. In other works, existing spaces are contrasted with imaginary spaces.

Brouwn does not publish any photographs of his work or any biographical or bibliographical details. he does not consent to giving interviews. such information detracts from the work itself –"it is deadwood", argues Brouwn, "the work itself provides the interviews, writes the biography." Brouwn has maintained this attitude since the beginning and for him it constitutes a part of his work "…it is material", he says…."

JOE C.THREWITT re. The Work's of STANLEY BROUWN:

There is one thing worse than these so-called artists producing senseless pieces of work involving little skill. That is getting some unassuming bystander to do the senseless creation for them, and for no reward. That's what Stanley Brouwn apparently does and why anyone would give him house room, let alone gallery space to exhibit such garbage, is amazing to say the least.

Probably if push came to shove, good things could be said for many of the so-called artists featured. But having looked at what Stanley Brouwn has been up-to, there seems nothing he has done that makes him anything other than a incredulous fantasist with cuckoo tendencies or appear to be someone on a substance that is probably banned in the civilized world given the bizarreness of his exhibitions.

Okay let's examine some examples of Mr Brouwn's antics:

Starting with; walking through an empty gallery so you; the unsuspecting punter can experience 'cosmic rays'... And yes they are invisible!

My first thought is; why would any gallery want to be associated with such banal thinking? More to the point; why would anyone want to see an empty gallery, especially if they have to pay for the privilege. Although I'm not actually sure if you are required to pay to view Mr Brouwn's non-work, I am sure I wouldn't waste my time trying and can't believe why anyone would.

If that isn't daft enough, what about his imaginary distance theorem? Having read about it, I still can't make head-nor-tale of what this dude Brouwn is on about. It's just absolute bilge. The man himself blabs on about some form of vertiginous reasoning whereby measurement becomes meaningless. With this nonsense being supported by masses of art-bollockese drivel, waffling on about some made-up unit of length named 'sb'. Someone please tell me what on earth is an ''sb' and why is this Art? I can only assume the gallery guys who allow this stuff over their threshold must be on the same wacky wavelength as Brouwn or may-be in receipt of some hefty funding from sources some would find questionable.

It seems apparent Brouwn has made a name for himself by exploiting this imaginary distance theorem and the bollockese that surrounds it. Accordingly he has been afforded exhibit space in some renowned galleries across Europe including Spain and Germany. Who'd a thought the Germans, whom we know like rules and a bit of discipline, would take to this old nonsense!

Nevertheless, as already mentioned; Stanley Edmund Brouwn's biggest piss-take has got to be his scam to get Joe Public to create hand-drawn maps from a to b and then exhibit them under some dodgy pretext that they somehow portray his idea of space and time.. ughh! He even has the audacity to claim these public spirited efforts for himself by scrawling his name on them. And even more laughable, or sad dependant on how you look at this, he claims signature ownership of pages left blank by persons he professes preferred to provide him with verbal directions. But probably in reality, told the weirdo bloke to 'foxtrot-oscar'.

So, let's ask the simple question; "Does Stanley Brouwn really produce works of Art?" and… Does his work *show imagination*?

No one can argue that Mr Brouwn has one-hell of an imagination in fact his world seems one big crazy fantasy. But to be classed as Art this imagination surely must show some skill combined with creative application. So Mr Brouwn although you have an odd imagination its not Art is just an odd imagination, that somehow you have been allowed to thrust upon us the general public.

Nevertheless, does Brouwn's work *involve any skill*? That seems a definite no-no to any reasonable person. Although a few of the members of the helpful public who have afforded their time to scrawl a map for the man…may-be!

With regard to the third element; Does Brouwn's work *possess beauty or ideas with emotional power*? Ha.. You've got to be having a laugh! If anyone considers this chap's work to hold any beauty or importance to anyone other than Brouwn himself, then this book is not for you… and you probably should be receiving help to restore some compos-mentis! This of course excludes gallery owners whom it appears would be happy to exhibit all forms of excrement if it were on a promise to make a buck.

The real shame is as mentioned within the back-story bollockese of Mr Brouwn. When in the early 1960's Brouwn allegedly destroyed and binned his works. Why-oh-why at this point in his life didn't a mate of his tell him to give-up and stop inflicting his vain weird nonsense's on hard working members of the public as an excuse for Art?...Apart from that... Stanley Edmund Brouwn's non-art is brilliant (only joking!).

Joe's Quote of Note for Mr Brouwn and his works (by others): *"You can fool all the people some of the time and some of the people all the time, but you cannot fool all the people all the time."* **Abraham Lincoln** *(attributed)*

CHAPTER 18

OSCAR TUAZON

O scar Tuazon is an American artist based in Los Angeles who works in sculpture, architecture, and mixed media.

Born: 1975, Seattle, Washington, United States
Education: Cooper Union
Patron: Charles Saatchi
Known for: Installation art, Sculpture   *Source Wikipedia*

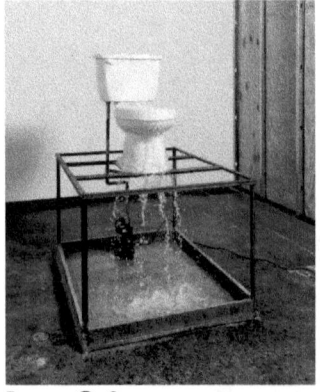

Image@s3.amazonaws.com

Oscar Tuazon and Eli Hansen's -

Toilet Sculpture (2014)

Toilet, steel, 68 x 36 1/4 x 47 1/4 inches.

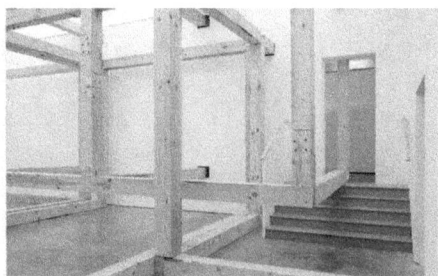

Photo Steve White

Oscar Tuazon's – 'My Mistake' Installation (2010)

EXAMPLES of ART- BOLLOCKESE*:-

Comments from 'Art Experts' re. The Work's of OSCAR TUAZON:

Extract from: www.theguardian.com "Sculpture of the Week (28 July 2010)"

" Oscar Tuazon's art may be vulnerable, but you'd never guess. His sculpture-cum-architecture has used raw slabs of concrete, steel and untreated wooden beams, bark-encrusted tree trunks and weighty metal chains. For his current installation, My Mistake, at London's ICA, the artist has assembled what looks like a massive climbing frame from tree-size pine beams. Almost too big for the gallery, one girder even bursts through a wall…..

…Inspired by what he calls "outlaw architecture", Tuazon channels the extreme DIY and freethinking of hippy survivalists who decide to go off-grid. If his industrial materials suggest a minimalistic stress on concept over making, he's just as interested in the physical side of sculpture. He is not afraid to get his hands dirty: working with riggers and technicians, he starts off with a sketch, chain-sawing wood, developing ideas and patching up problems on the hoof. From the impromptu-looking concrete slab that intersects the two-storey wooden frame of his 2009 work, Bend It Till It Breaks, to the neon strip light glowing two and a half metres up an untreated tree-trunk buttressed by planks in I Wanna Live, his structures have a rough-shod, improvised feel.

As muscular and uncompromising as it can first appear, Tuazon's work is ephemeral. Like the hippy idealists defining their environment on their own terms, the artist will always have to pack up and move on. Yet while they stand, pushing at walls and ceilings and taking over space, these makeshift constructions remind us of the imaginative struggle to make what we want of the world, no matter what rules and boundaries seem to press down on us…"

Extract from : www.frieze.com/article/oscar-tuazon:

" As one of the many artists currently engaged in appropriations of and tributes to their predecessors, Oscar Tuazon's approach is one of homage.

---

* **BOLLOCKESE** - Nonsensical verbiage or high-brow language used to communicate; unproven or biased opinion or an exaggerated truth; by a person who possesses or has pretensions of superior learning to project or promote items or concepts.

The Los Angeles-based artist's sculptural interventions arise via approximations of, and imagined conversations with, artists whose creative output have transformed aesthetic boundaries. Like his heroes, from Gordon Matta-Clark to wilderness survivalists, Tuazon's non-conformist approach to artistic practice plays at the juncture of architecture, sculpture and performance. For his solo exhibition 'dépendance', he employed architecture as both model and catalyst for an 'outlaw' ethos.

The show comprised a single work, *dépendance* (2012), an architectural replica of the gallery's façade and entrance. Within a few steps of walking into the space, visitors again encountered the exterior structure of the gallery – a white wooden frame, door and seven glass windows – creating a sense of déjà vu. A facsimile in both scale and materials, complete with the gallery's inconspicuous signage, the façade contrasted with the simple metal support structure surrounding it, recalling Tuazon's composite assemblies of building materials. Behind it, the gallery space lay open and empty, which subsequently directed one's attention back to the freestanding structure's bewildering presence and likeness to the original.

Tuazon's work can ostensibly be described as a series of encounters, or junctures, between independent parts working in a balanced yet tense interplay. Take his 2009 exhibition at Centre international d'art et du paysage in France, entitled 'Plie-le jusqu'à ce qu'il casse' (Bend it Until it Breaks), which involved a prodigious wooden frame built with pulleys that held horizontal concrete beams in suspension; or his large-scale wooden structure *Untitled* (2010), which weaved through the architecture of Kunsthalle Bern in Switzerland. With *dépendance*, Tuazon did not wholly abandon his assault against the existing site, but the force of his gesture was situated in the dislocation and disorientation one experienced when confronted with the uncanny reproduction. This disquieting consequence evoked the performative qualities of Tuazon's work, which often remained ancillary to his construction and materials.

In the exhibition's accompanying text, Tuazon called *dépendance* 'a cover version' of Glen Seator's *Approach* (1966–67) – a replica of the façade of San Francisco's Capp Street Project and a section of the abutting pavement, which Seator installed inside the non-profit art space. Along with Seator's intervention, Tuazon's text also cites Waylon Jennings's breakthrough album of cover songs. The comparisons bring Tuazon to consider the idea of the cover across music and artistic practice;

his reference to both artist and singer extends from a personal logic by which he defines them both as mavericks in their respective fields. By operating outside of, or insistently defying, prescribed conventions, Seator and Jennings fall within Tuazon's category of the 'outlaw'. His penchant for an outlaw attitude underscores the renegade attributes in his own work, which tends to be interpreted as abrasive, violent, defiant or confrontational. But his provocations are more willingly a matter of transcending artistic boundaries and codes…"

Extract form www.questia.com – "Structural Tension; Julian Rose on the Art of Oscar Tuazon" :

"…..Yet to look into Tuazon's work and find only a reinforcement of existing trends would be to miss an opportunity to move beyond the very binaries his work seems at first to reinforce. There is an undeniable aggression in Tuazon's work, as well as a distrust of architectural orthodoxy. He often speaks of his lifelong interest in alternative or "outsider" architectural movements, ranging from the ad hoc constructions of hippie communes to the portable and do-it-yourself shelters of hard-core survivalists. But whatever his interest in these precedents, Tuazon does not follow them completely outside the cultural establishment. His work still operates in, around, and between art and architecture. And while his work remains critical, it is tempered by a deep insight into the way these fields operate. Tuazon does not leverage abstractions such as "art" or "sculpture" in a blunt attack on an equally abstract notion of "architecture." Rather, he tunes his work to selectively relate certain trends, practices, and histories in each discipline to the other….."

 JOE C.THREWITT re. The Work's of OSCAR TUAZON:

Don't you think Oscar Tuazon should be better known as; 'Oscar's Plumbing & Building Services'? And there is nothing wrong with that. Plumbing and Construction Building are both honourable and worthwhile skills. Nevertheless, they should not be termed 'Art' no more than any recognised service provision. Okay..what if Telecommunication Engineers exhibited their junction boxes or Refuse Collectors the contents of their dust-carts. It just is what it is; functional services created for the purpose to which they were intended which in the main is domestic use. Not Art!

It has to be accepted some things produced by professionals in the execution of their daily tasks are visually pleasing. Take Architectural lay-outs or food prepared by those master-cheffy type people, some are truly amazing. But they are what they are; products made in the course of their work and although they now seem to fit what the art-bollockese intellectuals accept as 'Art', we must rue the day this happens as our galleries will then become just more showrooms, shops or restaurants... think about it!

Another thing; Why would anyone want to own a toilet system or a big wooden open plan structure created by Oscar when their local plumber or general builder could knock one up for the going rate, which I bet is far far cheaper and probably better constructed than Oscar's efforts.

The art-bollockese written about Mr Tuazon, claims his works portray the concept of 'outlaw architecture' whereby they suggest Tuazon sculptures, that are really structures, exhibiting; "..*a minimalistic stress on concept over making*".

Can you imagine what would happen if a building site foreman found his carpenters had built a house too bloody big...and when asked to explain they offered up.. "Gawd blimey guvnor don't you understand the *minimalistic stress on concept over making*"... Arse and kick comes into mind!

Another of Mr Tuazon's works which seems to defy all sense of understanding is his effort to build a reproduction of the entrance to a gallery within the gallery as an exhibit. The bollockese surrounding this so-called installation states that it creates a sense of "..*déjà vu*... *by operating outside of, or insistently defying, prescribed conventions*". I agree with this. Reproducing the outside of a building inside the same building does defy prescribed conventions. However, tell me this; why would anyone want to do it let-alone see it? And, why would a gallery think anyone would want to see it enough to allow such a structure to be erected with all the hassle it surely entailed?

Of interesting note is the recorded patron of Mr Tuazon's works; Charles Saatchi. Mr Saatchi as we know is fond of a bit of 'off-the-wall' art and is connected to other featured so-called conceptual artists. Therefore, it does seem to beg the question; Does he truly like this stuff or is he simply amusing himself (whilst enhancing his bank balance) by amassing odd-ball material then hyping it to increase its value? There is nothing illegal about this but it would be far more appreciated, by this commentator at least; if the artists chosen for patronage had obvious artistic flair and talent with no simplistic or bizarre traits. It has been said these marketing gurus that have changed the face of art three times. Therefore is it too much to ask for them to change it again and champion great artworks with visible complexities and skills that require no bollockese explanations?

Anyhow, getting back to Mr Tuazon and his so-called art structures, the question must be asked if they truly are 'good art' as the bollockese boys claim. As his installation obviously possesses some imagination, albeit non-conventional, and some technical skill as is necessary in the building of any structure. The only question that remains is whether the pieces created by Mr Tuazon are things of beauty or portray something of importance?

It is on this later point there is definitely a problem. Although Mr Tuazon may argue together with anyone associated with him and his installations that his works should be considered exceptional pieces of 'Art' and of significant importance, I'm afraid this man on the omnibus disagrees. They just aren't beautiful and any importance is lost because there simply isn't anything of any importance about them other than may-be a few tips to a DIY enthusiast.

The bollockese claims Mr Tuazon's structures, "*...can ostensibly be described as a series of encounters, or junctures, between independent parts working in a balanced yet tense interplay..*" But none of this is of importance to anyone, as you can find all of these descriptive words associated with items as mundane as sewer pipes. Nevertheless, sewer pipes in their proper setting are of course important to remove dross and waste. Therefore may-be Mr Tuazon's structures and their supporting bollockese could be considered as 'Art' by simple association...or Not!

Joe's Quote of Note for Mr Tuazon and his structures: *"Architecture is a visual art, and the buildings speak for themselves." **Julia Morgan***

CHAPTER 19

YVES KLEIN

Yves Klein (French pronunciation: [iv klɛ̃]; 28 April 1928 – 6 June 1962) was a French artist considered an important figure in postwar European art. He is the leading member of the French artistic movement of Nouveau réalisme founded in 1960 by art critic Pierre Restany. Klein was a pioneer in the development of performance art, and is seen as an inspiration to, and as a forerunner of, minimal art, as well as pop art. *Source Wikapedia*

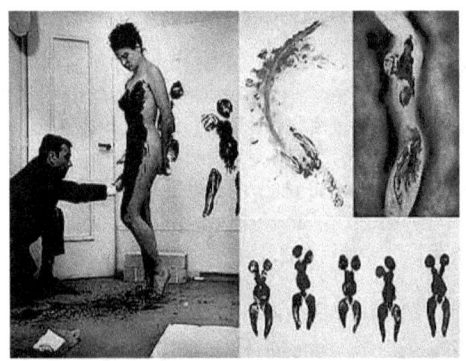

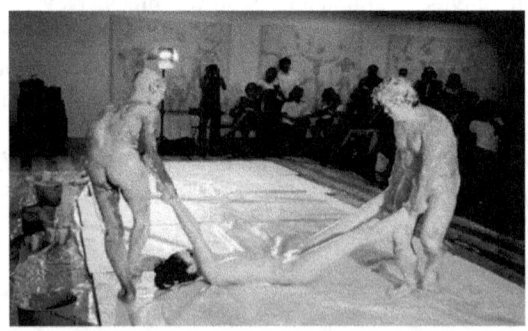

Images showing Yves Klien's Exhibition (1960)
Using naked models as paint brushes

EXAMPLES of ART- BOLLOCKESE*:-

Comments from 'Art Experts' re. The Work's of YVES KLIEN:

Extract from: www.bbc.co.uk/culture/story (28 August 2014)

"…For all his influence on conceptual art, though, Klein was most preoccupied with colour. As early as 1956, while on holiday in Nice, he experimented with a polymer binder to preserve the luminescence and powdery texture of raw yet unstable ultramarine pigment. He would eventually patent his formula as International Klein Blue (IKB) in 1960.

Before that, though, he made his name with an exhibition held in Milan in January 1957 that included 11 of his unframed, identical signature blue monochromes, one of which was bought by the Italian artist Lucio Fontana. This show ushered in what Klein called his "Blue Revolution", and soon he was slapping IKB onto all sorts of objects, such as sponges, globes and busts of Venus. Even his 'living brushes' dipped their flesh in IKB.

Art historians still debate the significance of Klein's use of ultramarine. For some, it represented a break with angst-ridden abstraction, which was popular in the wake of World War II. Painted mechanically using a roller, Klein's flat, blank monochromes seemed to rebuff expressionist art.

For other scholars, though, Klein's depthless monochromes and obsession with 'the void' can be understood as expressions of the threat of nuclear holocaust. "We absolutely must realise – and this is no exaggeration – that we are living in the atomic age," Klein once said, "where all physical matter can vanish from one day to the next to surrender its place to what we can envision as the most abstract."

Yet perhaps his love of blue is less specific and more profound. Klein was a pious Catholic, and in religious art blue often represents eternity and godliness. For instance, Giotto, whom Klein admired, was a brilliant advocate of blue. Klein's ultramarine monochromes are not overtly Christian, but he certainly used the sensuousness of IKB to

---

* **BOLLOCKESE** - Nonsensical verbiage or high-brow language used to communicate; unproven or biased opinion or an exaggerated truth; by a person who possesses or has pretensions of superior learning to project or promote items or concepts.

suggest spirituality. As he once said, "At first there is nothing, then there is a profound nothingness, after that a blue profundity."

Certainly, his rich, radiant monochromes share a singular characteristic: they all have a vertiginous quality that seems to suck us out of reality towards another, immaterial dimension. The effect of looking at them is not dissimilar to meditating upon a deep azure sky…"

Extract from: www.artinamericamagazine.com (*Magazine May 01, 2010*)

"…In 1948, at the age of 20, Yves Klein laid claim to the kingdom of the sky. Its presence hovers in the monochrome blue panels he began painting in 1955. But Klein's blue is not the pallid tint of the daytime sky. It is the dark, electric blue of the Paris sky at nine o'clock on a summer night, when the energy of the vanished day still resonates through the atmosphere, and the headlights of the traffic seem like sparks descending from above.

Klein's blue monochromes have the kinetic energy of van Gogh's *Starry Night*, all the more intense for being compressed into a single hue. His other paintings—some pink, some gold, some impressed with traces of the human body, some scarred by waves of flame—also offer moments of extraordinary beauty. Even as he was making these paintings, Klein staged a series of events rejecting conventional ideas of painting and sculpture. In 1958, he exhibited an empty gallery. In 1960 he published a fake newspaper. In 1962, he sold certificates for non-existent works of art. He is a forerunner, if not a founder, of installation art, conceptual art and institutional critique.

For Klein, painting and sculpture were means to a greater end. "My works are only the ashes of my art," he proclaimed in 1960. His goal was to transform first art, and then the world. Like Joseph Beuys a few years later, Klein saw himself as a shaman, an architect of souls, a Napoleon of the spirit. In the cold light of history, he can look like a charlatan, a raving narcissist alternating between megalomania and despair. But almost everyone who knew Klein seems to have considered him a genius…."

Extract from: www.theguardian.com- "Yves Klein and the birth of the blue" *Friday 13 May 2016* :

"....Klein is one of the most radical figures in postwar western art. He influenced minimal, conceptual and performance art, taking painting out of the frame, which he felt had imprisoned it for too long. His monochromes, hung several inches in front of the wall, were intended to saturate the viewer's space. Klein also blurred the boundaries between painting and sculpture by impregnating a range of objects, from sponges to plaster casts, with his signature blue.

In his "anthropometries", he helped naked female models smothered in paint to impress their moving bodies on large sheets of paper. He invented a number of other strategies to depersonalise and dematerialise the art object, including using fire and presenting empty space ("the void"), which he felt was pregnant with possibilities. Much of his work has a spiritual or transcendental quality. Given the importance of London in Klein's artistic development, a campaign has been launched to have an English Heritage plaque placed on the house in Cromwell Road. Perhaps it could be in International Klein Blue…"

Extract from: www.theguardian.com- "Yves Klein review – a superheated plunge into the wild blue yonders" *Thursday 20 October 2016* :

" Klein also created sculptures by sticking paint-soaked sponges on wooden sticks held in stone bases. For variety, he sometimes stained the sponge rose instead of blue. These floating sponges are an absolute delight, cool and beautiful and yet so simple I am seriously tempted to make one at home.

That would not be as easy as it looks, for Klein had a genius for intensifying colour. His earliest works in this lucid retrospective are small one-colour paintings that he started making at the beginning of the 50s and first exhibited in a Paris gallery in 1957, in a show called Propositions Monochromes. This was a revolutionary moment in art history. Across the Atlantic, the abstract expressionists were using colour in a completely free way. Their vision is superheated with sublimity and feeling, while Klein's monochromes are passive, silent, even slightly comic, as if playing with the potential absurdity of making art about nothing.

His simplification of art to the most uninflected of gestures – putting one colour evenly on a surface – is like the revolution in jazz that

Miles Davis announced in his 1957 album Birth of the Cool. Everything about Klein is almost ridiculously cool, including the formal suits he wears in all the nostalgic black and white performance photographs scattered through the show.

Another Miles Davis album, Kind of Blue, sums up Klein's next step. He fell in love with a deep ultramarine. Experimenting with chemistry, he perfected this radiant hue and patented it as IKB (International Klein Blue). Yet it is not just the blueness that is powerful. Klein devised a new method of suspending colour. Instead of using traditional oils, his paintings are made with raw pigment preserved in a specially developed synthetic gel. This is why they have lost none of their brightness and strength

The blue that saturates this exhibition is both repetitive and multitudinous. In some lights, it seems almost fluorescent. Up close, the blue is matt and rough, a suede-like surface. From afar, it is like a blue hole in the world. You could fall through it or dive in.

Blue has a long history of religious and spiritual meaning – and Klein saw an affinity between his blue paintings and the ultramarine skies in Giotto's frescoes in the Scrovegni chapel in Padua. Blue is also traditionally the colour of the Virgin Mary's robe. It is pure, heavenly and diving into it brings a release, a calm. This is therapeutic art.

Yet Klein's abstract immersions never leave the human body behind. His art was a physical performance – sometimes a dangerous one. His eerie Fire Paintings still have the whiff of mortal risk. He literally played with fire to make them, with firemen on standby and, it seems, joining in as collaborators. The scorched results look like brown and black images of cosmic events, black holes and nebulae, the shadow of an eclipse, the birth of the universe…"

 JOE C.THREWITT re. The Work's of YVES KLEIN:

It is reckoned Yves Klein (pronounced *Kle* by our French friends) was someone with special talent according to the art-intellectual elite. They claim he progressed from compiling one colour blobs (predominantly blue blobs) to painting naked bodies and rolling them over paper. Something like a human John-Bull printing set, if you're old enough to remember such things. The pictures produced naturally vary; relative of course to the hanging of the models 'threepenny-bits' if it's a lady model, and if it's a man, how much paint his 'old-chap' can splash about. Probably not much if it's a cold day!

It is noticeable *Monsieur Kle* liked to wear a business suit while painting his models. This was probably just a ploy to try and convince anyone interested in his nonsense that he wished to be taken seriously. Sorry to say, it would take much more than a suit to make his works credible to this commentator. It would probably be better (but not much) if he had shown the conviction of his ludicrous actions and worked in his birthday-suit. After a good day's work he could have then rolled-out a self portrait…yuk!

What seems lacking with *Mssr Kle's* so-called works of art, are like many of his ilk; 'effort and skill'. Also like many others before him, *Mssr Kle* has founded an 'ism' or (*'isme' in French*) as an excuse for the apparent lack of effort and skill. With his claim to art-fame being the bollockese term: Nouveau réalisme. And we all now know what's required to introduce such a new-ism! Acres of bollockese supporting an absurd concept which of course has been lovingly embraced by every lazy and unskilled paint operator out-there.

It is also of note, one of the bollockese articles that can be found on-line is headed *'The Absence of Art'*, which although seemingly obvious to this commentator, the article then goes on to quote some bloke called 'Pierre' who claims *Kle's* monochrome efforts (blobs of paint) *"..invoke Zen like contemplation".* This bollockese in support of *Yves Kle's* monochrome blob in orange resulted in it being exhibited at a top Parisian gallery. Which some would suggest; just goes to prove the adage of the importance of 'whom you know' (and can gush bollockese in your favour). This is not only important, but seemingly now a 'must' in the art-world if you want acclaimed recognition.

Those supporters of *Mssr Kle* will also argue that because he did what he did a good while ago, he should be applauded for his amazing innovative creations. This it is felt should be afforded no credence. Why should age and era be used as an excuse for lack of effort or skill? Also and more to the point; his unfortunate legacy was to inspire subsequent lazy and unskilful excuses for couch potato artists to copy his lead. There are now so many dabblers in paint claiming to be artists who just create child like daubs on the back of these 'isim-ists' (a new word courtesy of Joe C Threwitt) it seems shameful and a serious inhibitor to true artists with creative technical abilities.

Nevertheless, *Monsieur Kle* was truly embraced by the art establishment as the bollockese tells you. It seemed his 'painted nudes rolling on paper' exhibitions were immensely popular. So yes we are back to that old art trick that never seems to fail; nudity. I can safely bet my old dad's gold watch, the voyeurs at these exhibitions were not so interested in the finished creation as the creating. There does definitely appear to be a theme running here; it doesn't matter what old tosh is being exhibited, but if you care to throw in a bit of nonsense nudity with supporting arty-bollockese… it's a winner every time!

With regard to *Mssr Kle's* work being Art, as per the recognised definitions? Yes okay although there is little skill evident in the works of *Kle,* but nevertheless like any block of colour adorning your walls, it may be seen as an enhancement. As for his pictures created by painted naked bods gyrating on paper, the participants are probably having great fun enjoying their 15 minutes of fame. It therefore has to be accepted the end result which produces random daubs of colour, could loosely be termed as Art…but in this instance who really cares!

My summing up was going to end there, but there is no-way Joe public should be influenced that this chap *Kle* being labelled 'cool', as suggested by one of the art-bollockese commentators. Yes, it is impressive that *Mssr Kle* found a tinge of blue not previously used in painting from his chemistry set, and found some gel to increase the colours shelf-life. But, painting nudes in a waiters-suit and knocking out simplistic paintings consisting of one block of colour, is about as cool as his playing-with-fire efforts which probably would have benefited from a hose-down by the team of Firemen he had on stand-by. This arty-bollockese individual also equates *Mssr Kle's* work to being as 'cool' as the works of jazz musician Miles Davies. However, Jazz has layers of musical complexities that makes the music livelier.. Therefore please explain Mr arty-bollockese boff; how does this compare, in any way, to painting simple daubs in one colour..?

And.. **Joe's Quote of Note** for Yves Klien for his naked daubs:
" As long as people pay admission… to see a naked body rather than a naked mind, the drama will languish." **Bernard Shaw**

CHAPTER 20

HELEN MARTEN

Helen Elizabeth Marten is an English artist based in London who works in sculpture, video, and installation art. Marten studied at the Ruskin School of Drawing and Fine Art at the University of Oxford, 2005–2008 and Central Saint Martins, 2004.

Born: 1985, Macclesfield

Awards: Turner Prize , Hepworth Prize for Sculpture.

Education: Ruskin School of Drawing and Fine Art (2005–2008), Central Saint Martins. *Sourse Wikipedia.*

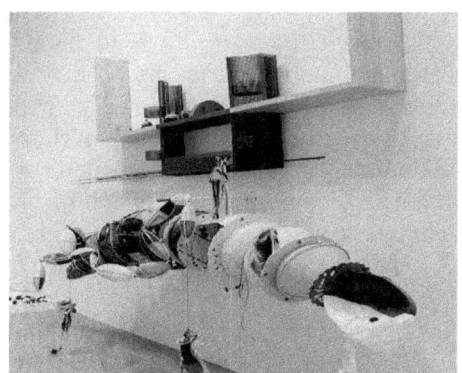

Image@www.standard.co.uk

Helen Marten - 'Night-Blooming Genera' (2016)
Forms part of the exhibition that was judged so exceptional it won her the turner prize accolade.

Steel; Aluminium; Model Board; Ash; Cherry; chipboard; sprayed MDF; blown glass; glazed ceramic; screen printed Latex; bucket; cast Resin; cast Jesmonite; stones; cast Rubber; flocked aluminium; gold leaf; cotton; nails; magnets; heating filament; lace; vinyl; twig; glass beaker; cast concrete; brass; Neoprene rubber; stitched and embroidered fabric; airbrushed steel; cardboard; sand; sugar; felt; oyster shell

Overall: 118 1/2 x 321 5/8 x 44 inches (301 x 816.9 x 111.8 cm)

EXAMPLES of ART - BOLLOCKESE* :-

Comments from 'Art Experts' re. The Work's of HELEN MARTEN:

Extract from: www.theguardian.com – "Helen Marten: from a Macclesfield garage to artist of the year " *Tuesday 22 November 2016* :

"...Helen Marten is having quite a year and, indeed, quite a career. Her first solo show in Britain was in 2012, at the Chisenhale in London, the seeding ground of bright young artists. Her work has twice been shown at the Venice Biennale, an exhibition of hers has just closed at the Serpentine in London, and last week she won the inaugural Hepworth prize for sculpture. She is in the running for the Turner prize, too (which she has actually won becoming the 2016 winner) – all at the age of 31...."

.... "The notion that the artist wants to be a public figurehead and immersed in spectacle is just nonsense for me," she says. "The artist has a responsibility to communicate in a way that is egalitarian in a world that is increasingly hermetic – but that's also the job of the institution and the curator. I love talking about my work – but I don't want to do it in a forum that is a corrupted, dumbed-down version of my words. No one wants to be paraphrased to sound like an idiot because that's accessible. That's depressing." She grins disarmingly. "Take note!"

As it happens, her work is not especially easy to read, and is devilishly hard to describe. Encountering a sculpture of hers, one first takes in a structure that might dimly recall an upturned desk, or a trough or a cradle. But then there's the endless detail, and your eye is drawn into a world of small things whose nature seems recognisable, but at the same time strange or strained: a match from a matchbook faces off with a small bell; ceramic pipes are draped with not-quite-socks; a coil of rope is topped with what looks like a fist-clenched ball of foil and a leaf. There are things that resemble jugs hanging from hooks; there are spoons flattened out into unspoonness; there are glass gherkins suspended from a metal framework as if about to be the subject of some kind of chemical experiment.

---

* **BOLLOCKESE** - Nonsensical verbiage or high-brow language used to communicate; unproven or biased opinion or an exaggerated truth; by a person who possesses or has pretensions of superior learning to project or promote items or concepts.

Walking round her recent exhibition at the Serpentine show, I was struck by what the objects have been put through – they are nailed, piled, folded, hooked, strung, pegged, pierced, slung, plaited, laced, zipped and dangled. At first it seemed to make no sense, but then, gradually, rhythm bounces off the objects, and one finds sense in the repeated, or near-repeated motifs – the matchsticks, which you might see stuck into piping; or the threads that you want to follow on their tangled, wound-up journeys.

If you submit yourself to this art – approaching the sculptures like free verse whose meaning you might rather absorb than decode – you realise you are in a place unlike any you've entered before, where a distinctive mind has messed with the world of objects and meaning, creating her own strange, compressed archaeology, which you are invited to expand into imaginary life.

I don't shop for things. I know what it is I am searching for

Her starting point, she tells me, is reading. "Before I touch anything in the studio, before I do anything tangible or physical, I spend three or four months reading and researching, but not with a specific end goal in mind. It could be fiction, theory, news, philosophy. I read a lot of poetry. The primary impulse more often than not is linguistic."…..

… Every move in her sculptures, every juxtaposition and careful placing can be precisely justified, she says, according to her own imaginative parameters – even if this exactitude may be lost on some of her viewers. "I feel I know with such clarity what it is and how it comes together and sometimes I'm patting myself on the back and feeling, 'This makes so much sense,' and you put it in the world and everyone says, 'It's like bric-a-brac.' And you just want to say, *fuck off*. For me this is the most logical thing. It's really a kind of humbling lesson doing public exhibitions, because sometimes people have no idea – and curators often don't get it."…"

Extract from: www.independent.co.uk – "Helen Marten wins Turner Prize for 'poetic and enigmatic' work" Monday 5 December 2016 :

"….Alex Farquharson, Tate Britain director and the chair of the judges, said Marten was making work which had "real longevity" and was using objects, forms and images in "a similar way to a poet using language".

"The judges were impressed by the complexity of the work, its amazing formal qualities, its disparate materials and techniques and also how it relates to the world... how it often suggests meaning, but those meanings are all in flux somehow. One image, one form becomes another," he said.

A spokesman for Tate Britain added that the jury "admire the work's poetic and enigmatic qualities which reflect the complexities and challenges of being in the world today"...."

Extract from: www.tate.org.uk – *"Turner Prize 2016: Helen Marten"* :

" Helen Marten uses sculpture, screen printing and her own writing to produce installations that are full of references, from the contemporary to the historical, and the everyday to the enigmatic. For the Turner Prize she brings together a range of handmade and found objects drawn from daily life and more unusual sources (including cotton buds, coins, shoe soles, limes, marbles, eggs, snooker chalk and snakeskin). Her collage-like gatherings of objects and images have a playful intent, creating poetic visual puzzles that seem to invite us into a game or riddle.

Marten's exhibition space is divided into three sections. Each suggests a workstation or terminal where some unknown human activity has been interrupted. When we encounter her installations, it is as if Marten asks us to become archaeologists of our own times, and to consider familiar items as if we are seeing them for the first time. In the process, these objects may become strange and abstract - 'husked down', Marten says, 'to geometric memories of themselves', that can be remodelled to give rise to new and unexpected stories or ideas.

Marten encourages us to look very closely at the items she makes and the materials she uses, and to reconsider the images and objects we surround ourselves with in the modern world..."

Extract from: frieze.com - "Helen Marten: My Influences (Skeumorphism)"

"...There's a huge piece of printed plastic hoarding currently clinging to the side entrance of London's King's Cross Station. The section closest to the commuter entrance is boldly marked with the station's name: a large, uncomplicated white font on a glossy red background. Redevelopments are underway so, amidst the inevitable skywards infrastructure, there's foot-to-ground activity happening everywhere. Approaching in a zig-zag from afar, sections of this signage disappear behind the fleshy chaos of pedestrian traffic, so it is possible that the only letters logged in a first conscious sighting of these words might be 'K' and 'I'. *Potassium Iodide.*

In a freefall of further abstracted musings, it is also possible to imagine that all the fluorescent activity unfolding behind this hoarding is in fact coupled with a radiological disaster, coagulating all rail connections and spewing nuclear mucus into London soils. The only barrier of protection is this shiny red wall, with that steady 'KI' lettering offering reassurance of the salty prophylactics on hand. More interesting, and still more absurd in this context, are the gradient shadows that border both top and bottom of the hoarding, alongside giant airbrushed discs that appear at rhythmic intervals across the entire length. It's graphic approximation on a huge scale: this red length is an I-beam, the discs are rivets, and those horizontal shadows markers of the scooped areas of space between the two steel flanges. As flattened moments of abc geometry, this almost-pictogram is hard to read in zoomed-in focus; only moving backwards do all the individual flatnesses align more three-dimensionally. It's a beautiful skeuomorphic thing, this enormously long and impossibly tall I-beam. There's a great conflation of information as material, a laminated rearrangement of that assumed magical tie between a word and a thing. The hoarding is probably plastic and attached quickly to wooden upright posts; these rivets are bigger than a face, and completely without materiality beyond their emulation of a structural function that we recognize. It's a series of trails, a type of comic approximation that grants imaginative license to the deciphering of all other nearby things. Translation is gorgeously wonky, but very simple too. Like the shutter-click on a camera phone, the mechanical integrity is synthetic but safe. So there's a doubly joyous moment in imagining a plastic briefcase passing by, itself stippled with dots of imitation leather grain; it's all part of our wonder of the atomic and everything looks good in nuclear light…"

 JOE C.THREWITT re. The Work's of HELEN MARTEN:

There is no doubt Helen Marten is a good person. She has won two eminent Art awards (Hepworth for Sculpture & Turner Prize Winner 2016). And on both occasions she has shared her winnings with her fellow contestants. This is most admirable and made me think twice of commenting on her works, albeit there is so much bollockese surrounding her installations of pots and pans and the like and her being a celebrated Turner Prize winner. However, while researching this young lady, what should turn up but a piece of gobbledegook, apparently written by Ms Marten, about something called '*Skeumorhism*'.

Well - **Skeuomorphism** *is the design concept of making items represented resemble their real-world counterparts.* **Skeuomorphism** *is commonly used in many design fields, including user interface (UI) and Web design, architecture, ceramics and interior design.*

Well I bet all you clever IT geeks out there are saying don't old Joe C. Threwitt know that. Well no, he doesn't and he doesn't want to. It is just another 'ism' bastardized from the Greek language that only someone trying to be an intellectual knob would ever dream of using. The simple reason being; you can say what it actually means in just a few simple words. So why use a word that is so obscure at least 90 percent of the world's population don't know what you're on about.

However, now that Ms Marten's works have gained immense public notoriety as a Turner Prize winner, let's examine her creations. It seems clear, like many so-called modern conceptual artists, Ms Marten has utilized items produced for functional living purposes to construct her works. With regard to the construction of her pieces, Ms Marten, again like so many of her peers, comes out with a load of bollockese that basically states she don't give a monkey's that others may think her works are a lot of old junk randomly joined together. The bollockese she has offered up claims the placement of the odds and sods making up her creations are carefully placed and, "*...can be precisely justified, she says, according to her own imaginative parameters.*" So actually it could be argued her works are indeed 'a load of old junk randomly joined together' as the justified placing can only ever be known to Ms Marten herself. Nevertheless, it seems we will never be listened to by the likes of Ms Marten as she allegedly maintains, "*This (her works) makes so much sense,' and you put it in the world and everyone says, 'It's like bric-a-brac.' And you just want to say, fuck off.*"

Therefore if Joe Public's comments are being dismissed, whose ears have the likes of Ms Marten's got?.. and more to the point.. Why?

The answer to these questions this seems blatantly obvious to this Joe; Once you allow radical teaching to be taught, the craziness will become the norm for the few who will become the new teachers of the many. Therefore it is inevitable, as per Richard A Rowland's quote; "*..the lunatics will take over the asylum*". To this commentator this is exactly where we are with the art-world. Therefore, art-bollockese is now the norm and to be expected alongside every modern conceptual work which viewed alone can-not explain it's self because it is a visual mess, or something so apparently lacking in skill any person with any self respect would be embarrassed to put on public display.

So much for the bollockese, but is Ms Marten's Turner Prize winning work really a piece of 'Art' as per the stated definitions?

I think it is fair to say her work does *show imagination.* There seems no argument about that, although it does seem to appear the result of random thought contrary to the bollockese commented.

Does her work *possess creative skill*?

Again I believe it is fair to say there may be some. This is because there does appear to be much tying, gluing and sticking to enable Ms Martens bric-a-brac works to hang or stand as the case may-be.

How about the final requirement of *possessing some form of beauty or message of significant importance*?

That to Joe C Threwitt is a definite No! Junk tied or glued, even if adorned with sequins, does not convince anyone of reasonable cerebral functions that it is a thing of beauty. With regard to having any message of importance, surely anyone not radicalized by any accompanying words would see it for what it is; meaningless non-sense. Having said that, her work is probably good fun to create in a class-room run by modern teachers, whom like so many, have themselves been taught that Art now includes everything including the kitchen sink or your mum's old plunger. What do you reckon; I bet this critique of her associated bollockese will earn a big "fuck off" from the lady!

Joe's Quote of Note for Ms Marten and her Turner Prize pals:

"Skill without imagination is craftsmanship and gives us many useful objects…Imagination without skill gives us modern art." **Tom Stoppard**

EPILOGUE

(Art-BOLLOCKESE 1-20)

If Joe C. Threwitt MA can make you see anything, it is this: Art Bollockese is now more important than actual Art. Passed Turner Prize winners including Helen Marten and Tracey Emin have seemingly proved this. No one is seeing the creations exhibited for what they are, but what you are being influenced or told they are. Without the accompanying art-bollockese these exhibits would, and should be viewed and assessed without explanation. These works would then be taken for what they truly display, which in the main are childlike constructs. So simplistic that standing on there own without any bollockese they are just inane concepts.

This book, and others that may follow, has come about because bollockese, and especially art-bollockese, has become so endemic within the art establishment it now seems pretty clear; bollockese and its championing of 'ism's' have increasingly eroded any requirement for artistic skill and provided an excuse to produce simplistic trash. So-much-so, the majority of modern / contemporary artists rising to notoriety, now arguably do so, on the back of marketing bollockese rather than any obvious skill in their creations.

There is no doubt the views of Joe C. Threwitt MA will not be appreciated by all. Especially those whose works rely on bollockese, or persons employed writing or gushing the stuff. Nevertheless, it is felt the balance now needs some redress with some sanity being restored to the arts which has become increasingly bizarre.

It is of global acceptance that appreciation of art is and should always be; 'in the eye of the beholder'. Joe C. Threwitt MA is not disputing this. However, what is being questioned here is: *Are we actually seeing Art in its true sense, or has the word become so bastardized by the art-establishment 'absolutely anything' with accompanying bollockese can now be considered Art.*

Therefore, although some may argue Joe is just a dinosaur with out-of-date perspectives. Joe will passionately deny this, as all that is being sought is some redress of balance to ensure artistic skill is not smothered by the absurd.

Accordingly, Joe accepts Art-Bollockese is not just reserved for the ridiculous pieces as those featured, it also accompanies great works including those created by the recognised masters. Nevertheless, Joe will also argue such drivel is not needed and actually detracts viewers from forming their own opinions and pleasure from the creations.

A good example of this can be found in reference to one of Joe's favourite works by the truly renowned artist; Kandinsky. Yes that's right; the Russian chap who produced works that were definitely obscure and abstract. So maybe ...Joe ain't such a dinosaur! The particular Kandinsky being referred to is called: *Composition VIII (1923)*. This painting is colourful and although abstract, the technical brilliance is there for all to see, but like all art it is not everyone's cup-of-tea. Nevertheless, there is no question this painting ticks all the boxes with regard to being a 'Work of Art'. Therefore, one would suggest and Joe certainly would, there is no requirement for any bollockese to accompany this picture. But yep.. they gush it out.. just have a read of this nonsense:

" *Composition VIII provides a good illustration of the 'inexhaustible variable' nature of the circle within a formal arrangement of geometric shapes. The circles range from a quite bubble...to the noisy solar form of the concentric rings...The contact of the acute angle of a triangle with the circle is no less powerful in its effect than that of the finger of God with the finger of Adam in Michelangelo's painting. By drawing this analogy, Kandinsky gives the meeting of these forms a cosmic significance.* "

It therefore seems clear, Art-Bollockese is not just employed for marketing new-wave bizarre works, but used by intellectuals bluffing out some improvable concept about any piece of art they wish to influence with their self-indulgent crankiness.

It is also of increasing note once an artist has reached public notoriety, usually by slick marketing, all works created by that artist become valued as if they hold the same ascetic worth as the one work that brought them into the lime-light. However, we all know artists like all humans have off-days with many of their final creations turning out to be mediocre to say the least.

Accordingly, it's further claimed by Joe C. Threwitt, Art-Bollockese used in the hyping of an artist has created the ridiculous situation where the artist is valued rather than their art. Even the great masters have knocked out rubbish, but we now value them the same as their good efforts, simply because they bear the masters' name. This only happened in the Arts and this Joe claims is due to what is conveyed by art-academic bollockese rather than any true visual interpretation.

So, there you have it, Joe C Threwitt's views on twenty so-called artworks and their associated bollockese. It is also of significant note that in *the real world*; there are far more people that think like Joe than think like conceptual artists. So remember this before you 'diss' the views expressed. Therefore if you believe Joe has hit the nail on the head or alternatively feel he is missing something, let us know by tweeting …. *joe@art-bollockese*. Your support will ensure Joe C. Threwitt MA will be back with another volume of equally crackpot creations and their associated ***Art- Bollockese***.

Joes Quote of Note to conclude volume 1 of Art Bollockese is:
"Bollockese is the language of Intellectual Bluffers and the Inept with Indulgent Egos."
Joe C. Threwitt MA

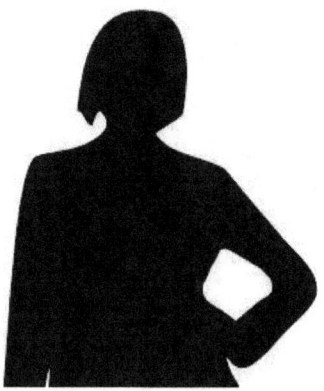

Joella Charlotte Threwitt MA
Better known as 'Average-Joe' to her pals:

Joe has been writing since she was 7 years old and since leaving college her primary published works are in pamphlet form held by HMIR. Although happily separated, Joe has 2.4 children and drinks no more than 14 units of alcohol per week ... allegedly! Joe thinks hard work is the only way to 'honestly' get ahead and therefore claims she watches just 2 hours 49 minutes of television a day. Joe is a pet owner and pays off her credit-card bill in full each month because she is permanently worried about being able to maintain her standard of living. Joe prior to becoming the champion of common sense was employed within the public sector where she held an opinionated role. Joe spends 23 minutes and 54 seconds commuting to work on her local omnibus. Joe is 5ft 3ins tall and weighs approx. 65kg. Joe claims to have sex 1.3 times a week in the winter but less in summer due to premature flushes. Joe loves all types of art that shows some element of skill in its creation. However, Joe doesn't like to listen to, or read bullshit ... other than her own!